The New Americans
Recent Immigration and American Society

Edited by
Steven J. Gold and Rubén G. Rumbaut

A Series from LFB Scholarly

Latino Families Broken by Immigration
The Adolescents' Perceptions

Ceres I. Artico

LFB Scholarly Publishing LLC
New York 2003

Library of Congress Cataloging-in-Publication Data

Artico, Ceres I. (Ceres Ildebrando), 1959-
  Latino families broken by immigration : the adolescent's perceptions /
Ceres I. Artico.
    p. cm. -- (New Americans : recent immigration and American
society)
Includes bibliographical references and index.
  ISBN 1-931202-63-X (alk. paper)
  1. Parental deprivation. 2. Attachment behavior in children. 3.
Adolescent psychiatry. 4. Hispanic American teenagers--Mental
health. 5. Hispanic American teenagers--Social conditions. 6. United
States--Emigration and immigration. 7. Central America--Emigration
and immigration. I. Title: Adolescent's perceptions. II. Title. III. New
Americans (LFB Scholarly Publishing LLC).
  RJ507.P37A78 2003
  362.7'089'68073--dc21

2003003569

ISBN 1-931202-63-X

Printed on acid-free 250-year-life paper.

Manufactured in the United States of America.

Table of Contents

Acknowledgements

I would like to thank Dr. Linda Seligman, Dr. Evelyn Jacob, Dr. Suzanne Denham, Dr. Gerald Wallace, and Dr. Donald R. Gallehr from George Mason University. Their support, knowledge, and valuable feedback helped me achieve my goals and complete this project.

Thanks to the staff at the Center for Multicultural Human Services, who helped me identify potential participants for this project, and in particular, to its director, Dr. Dennis Hunt, who generously allowed me to use the rooms and resources at the Center .

Thank you to all the participants and their families. This book was made possible only because of their willingness to trust their experiences and thoughts with me.

Finally, I thank my family and friends. Without their patient listening to my doubts and fears this project would never happen.

Introduction

Piecemeal immigration is common among families in poor and war-stricken countries. During the 1980's, Latino immigrants often left their children with extended family and immigrated to the United States. This study explored the experiences, perceptions, and memories of Latino adolescents and young adults reunited with their biological parents after prolonged separation during childhood because of piecemeal immigration patterns. The main hypothesis was that these children's interpretation of the parents' departure as abandonment or as sacrifice shaped their internal working models of self and others. Such representational models, in turn, predisposed these children to develop specific affective, cognitive, behavioral, and relational patterns. Attachment theory provided the conceptual framework for this study.

Three male and four female Latino adolescents, ages 15 to 19, described their experiences, reactions to, and memories of the separation from and reunification with their parents during in-depth interviews. After each interview they participated in an experiential activity with a sand tray. The interviews were audio taped, transcribed, coded and analyzed, and the sand tray constructions were photographed and analyzed.

The context leading to the parent's departure; the family's interpretation of parents' actions; the parents' dependability as providers during the separation; and the quality of communication in these families upon reunification influenced how these children perceived the parents' immigration. The way love and affection was expressed by parents and caretakers; the marital status of the parents, and the children's perception of adults as supportive or critical influenced their representational model of self. The way families handled the parent's departure, the characteristics of the child's relationship with parents and caretakers, and exposure to trauma and losses influenced the participants' internal working model of others. All these factors influenced how these children negotiated developmental tasks and life challenges and how these families handled the process of reunification. The two main factors that increased the distress among these families were ignorance about children's needs and poor communication patterns.

Professionals in the mental health and educational fields can help these families integrate their experience and rebuild broken relationships by facilitating communication, recognizing and validating their fears and needs, and providing education about the process of separation and reunification among family members. Further investigation and research on this topic can benefit Latino and other immigrants and refugees with a similar history.

CHAPTER 1

Patterns of Immigration in Families

A common pattern of immigration among Central American families is that the mother, father, or both parents will come to the United States by themselves, leaving their children in the care of extended family in the country of origin. Usually, it is not until a few years later that the parents are able to bring the children to the U.S. The purpose of this study is to better understand how Central American immigrant children give meaning to and integrate their history of prolonged separation and reunification with their parents in the U.S. due to piecemeal patterns of immigration.

The U.S. is currently facing the largest wave of immigration since the turn of the 20[th]century. Of the 18 million immigrants coming to the U.S. between 1971 and 1996, nearly 7 million (or 39% of all immigrants) have been Hispanics. For the past two decades, people from Central and South Americans have represented a large percentage of those seeking a better or safer life north of the border. According to the U.S. Bureau of the Census Statistical Abstracts for the United States (1996), over 1.3 million Central Americans and more than 1 million South Americans arrived in the U.S. in the 1990's (Cafferty & Engstrom, 2000).

> Hispanic Americans are one of the fastest growing demographic groups of the U.S. population. The Hispanic American population increased 53% from 1980 to 1990, and 27% from 1990 to 1996. By the year 2005, Hispanic Americans will surpass Blacks as the largest "minority group", and by 2010, Hispanics will outnumber the nation's Blacks,

Asian Americans, and American Indians combined.
(Hernandez, 1999, p. 3.)

Prior to 1975, immigrants from Central America were few.
However, beginning in the mid- and late 80's, mainly due to political
conflict and civil war, these numbers increased significantly and
continue to remain high. In 1995 for example, El Salvador and
Guatemala accounted for more than 50% of the legal immigrants from
Central America (Arroyo, 1997). The numbers of those who enter and
remain illegally in the country are very high, possibly surpassing those
of legal status. Although there is no official data on the number of
illegal immigrants living in the U.S., the Immigration and
Naturalization Services (INS) estimates that between 3 and 5 million
persons are in the U.S. illegally, with Hispanics making up more than
two-thirds of the undocumented immigrant population. Mexicans
comprise 50% of the entire illegal immigrant population, El
Salvadorans account for 6.7% of them, followed by Guatemalans, with
3.3% of all illegal immigrants current living in the U.S. Again,
according to the INS estimates, between 138,000 and 207,000 Latin
Americans enter the U.S. illegally every year (Cafferty & Engstrom,
2000).

One in every five children currently living in urban areas in the
U.S. is either an immigrant or the child of immigrant parents, with the
majority of immigrants being either Asian or Hispanic. The large
majority of immigrants settle in only a few areas. Ninety percent of all
Hispanic Americans in the U.S., for example, live in only 10 states
(Guerra, 1999; Hernandez, 1999). In 1990, the Washington D.C. area
ranked seventh in number of first- and second-generation immigrant
children, with over 15% of all children being first or second generation
immigrants (Hernandez & Darke, 1999). The authors define first
generation immigrants as the first children to be born in the United
States, whereas second generation immigrants are their offspring.

Family separation due to a piecemeal (1) pattern of immigration is
quite common, not only for Latinos, but also for African and Asian
immigrants, especially among those with limited resources (Gilad,
1990). There is no data available on the percentage of immigrants that
fall within such patterns of immigration (Personal communication,

Census Bureau and Office of Immigration and Naturalization Services, 1999). However, from looking at the very limited existing literature on the topic, considering informal observations of practitioners working in mental health and educational fields, and from my own professional experience, this seems to represent a widespread and important phenomenon among immigrant families. One of the few studies to mention this problem seems to confirm this assumption. In a survey with 153 Latina domestic workers living in California, researchers found that of the 75% who had children, 40% reported to have at least one child still living back in their country of origin. Among women with less secure jobs and life styles, that percentage was as high as 82% (Hondagneu-Sotelo & Avila, 1997). Even though this sample is small and limited to one type of worker, it does cast some light on the likely magnitude of the problem.

Such a pattern of immigration is neither an American phenomenon nor is it new. For many decades in the United States, Caribbean and African American women from the South have left their offspring "back home" while they migrate North to secure employment (Hondagneu-Sotelo & Avila, 1997). In England, during the wave of immigration from the Caribbean between 1955 and 1960, although parents took 6,500 children with them, they left over 90,000 children behind (Lowenthal, 1972). For those immigrants, very much like the stories told by contemporary Central American immigrants in the U.S., the length of separation greatly exceeded their initial expectations because the length of time needed to secure occupational and economic stability was grossly underestimated by the newcomers (Arroyo, 1997; Hondagneu-Sotelo & Avila, 1997).

A common pattern of immigration among Central Americans is that the mother, father, or both will come to the U.S., leaving the children in the care of grandparents, aunts, older siblings, and as a last resort, paid childcare. Once the mother or the parents get settled (which may take as long as 10 or 12 years), they will send for the children left behind. Often, by then the mother has remarried or co-habits with a new partner and has children born from this new relationship. This piecemeal pattern of migration among families from Central America influences the child's perception of the family and creates unique challenges for those children and their families (Arroyo, 1997). The child or adolescent now has the difficult task of adapting to a fairly unknown mother (and often a stepfather and half-siblings), as well as a new language, culture, social norms, and educational system. They also need to cope with the loss and separation from the surrogate parent, compounded, of course, by the developmental task of individuation, if they arrive as adolescents (Glasgow & Gouse-Sheese, 1995).

The influx of immigrants from Central America, caused especially by the outbreak of civil unrest and war in those countries in the past 20 years, has placed that population among one of the most visible in large metropolitan areas, such as in the Washington D.C. area. Among this population, piecemeal immigration is a prevalent pattern, creating unique dynamics and needs in these individuals and families. Ironically, despite its prevalence and importance, this issue has been virtually ignored by researchers.

Studies on the impact and specific difficulties of family separation due to immigration are almost non-existent (Arroyo, 1997). Yet, such difficulties are fairly common among immigrants, playing a very significant part in the lives of people with such history. In a clinical sample of Central American immigrant children, for example, symptoms of psychopathology were directly related to war-related trauma, family separation, disruption of social networks and education, and impoverishment (Arroyo, 1997; Masser, 1992). In working with these children I often notice that children who experienced separation have difficulty trusting and relating to their parents and feel angry for being treated by them as if they were younger than their actual age.

These children report that their parents tend to relate to them in the same way they did prior to the separation, without realizing that they are now much older and have different needs. It seems that because the parents were not present to witness the children's process of maturation, they have difficulty relating to them as they reunite years later. Separated children also feel unable to openly talk to their parents about their sadness over the loss of the surrogate caretaker and their ambivalence about coming to the U.S. Many report resentment once they realize that their parents are much poorer than they expected, and as the parents juggle two or three jobs, they have little or no time for their families. Life in the U.S. turns out to be a lot harder and lonelier than they expected (Glasgow & Gouse-Sheese, 1995). Such children have to negotiate the process of individuation, which is characteristic of adolescence, and at the same time try to connect to a parent they barely know (Blos, 1967). If these children express sadness and grief over the loss of their previous caretaker (often the maternal grandmother or grandparents), it may be seen as ingratitude and lack of recognition for the parents' sacrifice. Finally, such children are often faced with the need to adapt to a minority or lower social class status compared to what they were accustomed in their country of origin.

CONCEPTUAL FRAMEWORK

Childhood experiences are powerful in shaping, and often determining, who we become. This view, combined with my experience of working with immigrant children separated from their mothers in childhood, made me increasingly interested in attachment theory. That theory provides a useful framework to understand how a person relates to others, how self-concept and personality traits develop, and the role that attachment patterns play in the development of psychopathology. Therefore I used attachment theory as my main conceptual framework in approaching this project.

According to this theoretical approach, the specific ways one relates to the self and to others throughout life has its roots in the quality and characteristics of the relationship to the main caretaker in childhood, as well as in how people perceive, interpret, and integrate the memories of that relationship. From that perspective, predictable intra-psychic and inter-relational patterns, particular personality traits, and the risk to develop psychopathology will emerge (Ainsworth, 1984, Ainsworth, 1991; Colin 1996b).

Studies on attachment show a positive correlation between disruption of attachment in childhood and mental illness, as well as proneness to develop conflictual and unsatisfying interpersonal relations in adulthood (Berman & Sperling, 1994; Brenan & Shaver, 1995; Feeney & Noller, 1996). As people grow up, they tend to interpret and integrate their previous experiences with significant others using cognitive schemas and strategies that help them make sense of reality, create a consistent and coherent sense of self, and keep emotional distress at manageable levels. Such strategies and efforts to give meaning to internal and external reality are influenced not only by individual characteristics, but also by cultural and sub-cultural (i.e. familial) values and beliefs (Greenberg & Speltz, 1988; Grossman & Grossman, 1990; Harris & Bifulco, 1991; Hazan & Shaver, 1987).

Adolescence is one of the developmental stages when the attachment system is under revision, as individuals try to resolve issues of separation and individuation from the parents and family of origin to start establishing emotional connections to potential partners (Blos, 1967; Kroeger, 1996). If, on one hand, this makes the understanding of the participant's world in this project more complex, it also represents a unique challenge and opportunity to witness the unfolding of a fascinating process with all its conflicts and potential for resolution.

I used these concepts and theories (attachment, individuation process in adolescence, and cultural norms and values) to build a template that guided me in approaching this project. Like pieces of a puzzle, I kept these different concepts in mind as I designed the interview guide, the types of data to be collected, and the methods to analyze the data.

In this study I tried to obtain a first-hand account of how adolescents and young adults who were separated from their mother, father, or both during their childhood later conceptualized and integrated their experience at a cognitive and emotional level. My main hypothesis was that there was a core conflict in how children separated from their parents made sense of the parent's decision to leave. They struggled between seeing it, on one hand, as abandonment, and on the other, as a sacrifice the parents did for the family and the children's welfare. These two views are often mediated by individual differences, and influenced by family and cultural values and beliefs. The way we interpret the behaviors of important persons in our lives helps us shape how we see ourselves: known in attachment theory as our internal working model of self and others. Such representational or internal working models, in turn, often predispose individuals to certain patterns of affect, cognition, and behavior, ways of relating to others, and risk for developing emotional problems.

The specific questions I hoped to answer through this project were:

1. What meaning did young Central American immigrants separated from their parents in childhood give to the experience of separation?
    a. How did they explain to themselves the parents' decision to immigrate and leave them behind?

b. Was there a conflict between how they integrated the experience at the cognitive versus at the emotional level?
c. Was there a common meaning given by the participants to the experience of being left and to the decision made by the parent? If so, what were some of the commonly shared cultural, community, familial, and individual characteristics?

2. What was the impact of separation on these participants' representational or internal working model of self? If there was indeed a dichotomy between conceptualizing the separation as *abandonment* versus *sacrifice*, what role did it play in the participants' internal working model of self?

3. What was the impact of separation on these participants' representational or internal working model of others?
a. If there was indeed a dichotomy between conceptualizing the separation as *abandonment* versus *sacrifice*, what role did it play in the participants' internal working model of others?
b. If there was indeed a dichotomy between conceptualizing the separation as *abandonment* versus *sacrifice*, what part did it play in the participants' current relationship with their parent(s)?
c. How did this life experience and its interpretation by the participants impact their emotional development? Did it place them at risk to develop psychological problems?

Due to the nature of qualitative research, however, other themes, unexpected at the time this project was designed, continued to emerge as the study evolved and the data were analyzed. It also became clear that not all elements for analysis of the sand trays were relevant for the purposes of this research project. Therefore, only selected methods were used. Further details on additional themes and selection of data analysis methods will be provided in chapter 3.

Below are some of the terms and constructs I used throughout this project:

Separation: The physical distance of the child from the mother, father, or both, due to the parent(s) immigration to the U.S., while the child remains in the country of origin.

Reunification: The event and process of being reunited (and sharing residence) with the biological mother, father, or both, in the United States, after spending considerable time in the care of a surrogated caretaker in the country of origin.

Internal working models or representational models of self and others: Representational or working models are the cognitive and affective maps of self, others, and of relationships. Representational models include "feelings, beliefs, expectations, behavioral strategies, and rules for directing attention, interpreting information, and organizing memory." (Colin, 1996b, p. 19).

Transnational motherhood: mothers who leave their children behind and immigrate to wealthier countries seeking employment. Pressured by need, these mothers' priority changes from being with their children to providing for them, so as to ensure these children's chances to survive. According to Hondagneu-Sotello and Avila (1997), "Latina immigrant women who work and reside in the U.S. while their children remain in their country of origin constitutes one variation in the organizational arrangements, meanings, and priorities of motherhood" (p. 548).

CHAPTER 2

Review of Supporting Theories

Attachment theory, individuation in adolescence, and Latino culture are the three main topics reviewed and used as a guide in designing and carrying out this project. In addition, a review of relevant previous research on piecemeal patterns of immigration will be presented in this chapter.

ATTACHMENT THEORY

I used the tenets of attachment theory as the conceptual framework for this project. According to this theoretical approach, the specific ways one relates to self and others throughout life has its roots in (1) the quality and characteristics of the relationship to the main caretaker in childhood, and (2) in how, as adults, we perceive, interpret, and integrate the memories of that relationship. Those two main factors will determine people's basic attachment styles and their core personality traits (Berman & Sperling, 1994).

Historical Perspective

John Bowlby (1907-1980) was the first proponent of attachment theory. He called "attachment system" the complex constellation of feelings and behaviors that seemed to function as a system to protect infants by keeping them close to their mothers (Hazan & Shaver, 1987). As a psychiatrist working at the Tavistock clinic, in London, Bowlby observed that children separated from their caretakers for different lengths of time went through a predictable series of emotional reactions: protest, despair, and detachment. In the 1970's, Mary Ainsworth did extensive research on attachment of children to their main caretaker (mostly their mothers), which led to the classification and operationalization of attachment in children. Bowlby, Ainsworth, and many of the early researchers and theorists of attachment focused their work on early childhood and on the toddler's relationship with the main caretaker.

It was not until about 15 years ago that attachment in adolescence and adulthood gained attention in the literature. Adult attachment is conceptualized from three main lines of empirical inquiry. Developmental psychology examines attachment throughout the life span, using the methodology developed by Ainsworth and her followers. The socio-psychological line of inquiry investigates the relationship between early relationship with the main caretaker, attachment style, and its influence on how one negotiates the outside world, as represented by interpersonal relations, relationship with religious beliefs, and one's approach to work. Finally, researchers looking at attachment from a clinical perspective compare normative to clinical populations, in an effort to further understand the relationship between attachment styles and mental illness (Berman & Sperling, 1994).

Main Definitions in Attachment Theory

"Attachment is the enduring affective bond characterized by a tendency to seek and maintain proximity to a specific figure, particularly when under stress" (Colin, 1996b, p. 7), and its main function is to seek and provide protection. The attachment figure is a secure base from which to explore. Infants, for example, will play and explore their surroundings, but will seek periodic contact (look in the direction of, come closer to, or "touch base") with the attachment figure. Attachment is an "independent behavioral system, equivalent in function to other drive-behavioral systems, such as feeding, mating, and exploration" (Berman & Sperling, 1994, p.5). It is a goal-corrected behavior, in which cognitive and emotional schemata are used to induce the two parties to modify their behaviors so that they more closely reflect each person's needs and desires. "Attachments exist over time and across relationships...[and are] comprised of a genetically determined behavioral system, a mental representation of attachment relationships, a particular relationship history, and a specific environmental context" (Berman & Sperling, 1994, p. 14).

There are significant differences among the concepts of attachment, bonding, and relationships. Attachments are long lasting and directed to a specific, non-replaceable person: the attachment figure. Whereas relationships can be short or long-lived, and represent a two-way interaction, attachments have a protective function and are unidirectional, representing the bonding of the child towards the attachment figure (Ainsworth, 1991). Whereas the child is "attached" to the caretaker, adults develop "affectional bonds" to their own children and other adults, such as spouses and siblings. Being attached implies needing the other for protection and survival, whereas bonding implies a more egalitarian interdependency, in which adults take turns in providing protection and comfort to each other. Regulated by internal representational models, adults develop a tendency to "make substantial efforts to seek and maintain proximity to and contact with one or a few specific individuals who provide the subjective potential for physical and/ or psychological safety and security" (Berman & Sperling, 1994, p. 8).

Mary Ainsworth systematically observed infants and their mothers in their natural environment and in laboratory situations and found that children's behavior fell within three main attachment types: *secure*, and two types of insecure attachment, *avoidant* and *resistant*. Briefly described, Ainsworth found that when under stress, securely attached babies sought their mothers for protection, accepted their comfort and, after some time, resumed the play and exploration of the environment. Insecure babies, however, did not seek or use the attachment figure effectively to decrease stress. Avoidant babies acted as if the attachment figure was not important (although their biological measures of stress were comparable to that of secure babies), whereas resistant babies displayed anxious and mixed feelings, including anger towards the caretaker (Ainsworth, Blehar, Waters, & Wall, 1978). These laboratory experiments are commonly referred in the literature as the "Strange Situation". Later, Main identified a fourth type: *disorganized-disoriented* attachment patterns, usually seen in severely abused children (Greenberg & Speltz, 1988). The classification of attachment types used by George et al. (1996) parallels that used by

Ainsworth in toddlers. George et al. (1996) identified four possible classifications of the adult's state of mind in relation to attachment: *Secure, dismissing, preoccupied* and *unresolved* (Colin, 1996b; George, Kaplan, & Main, 1996).

Key Concepts in Attachment Theory

Representational or working models are the cognitive and affective maps of self, others, and of relationships. Representational models include "feelings, beliefs, expectations, behavioral strategies, and rules for directing attention, interpreting information, and organizing memory." (Colin, 1996b, p. 19). Our childhood experiences, particularly our relationship with the main caretaker, will influence how we will direct our attention. We will focus particularly in those aspects of reality that confirm the schemata we have already formed, a process known as *defensive exclusion*. Defensive exclusion is a cognitive process of ignoring incoming information that "when accepted in the past, has led the person concerned to suffer more or less severely" (Bowlby, 1980, p. 65). This strategy of reading and interpreting the external reality contributes to easier assimilation and lowered stress. "Like repression, defensive exclusion is regarded as being at the heart of psychopathology" (Bowlby, 1980, p. 69).

Once formed, working models tend to maintain their coherence and patterns for organizing information, setting the stage for future interactions with others. This process contributes to the self-perpetuating characteristics of representational models. Although working models are very resistant to change due to their self-fulfilling characteristics, life events and environmental circumstances have the potential to change early patterns of attachment. A positive relationship with mentors, relatives, therapists, and spouses can help create a stable and secure pattern of attachment in a person with a history of stressful or neglectful relationship with his caretaker during childhood. On the other hand, disruption, losses, and conflict in later life can contribute to increased display of insecurity, anxiety, and withdraw in a person previously operating under healthy and positive working models of self and others.

There are clear patterns of relating that stem from internal representational models, but this is by no means a linear or simplistic phenomenon, especially in adolescence and adulthood, where one's self-concept is intertwined and influenced by multiple variables. Relationships with siblings, relatives, peers, and mates will influence the individual's representational model, and there is some evidence that people may relate to others using two or more models of self and of the attachment figure simultaneously (Feeney & Noller, 1996; Bowlby, 1973). Finally, if an individual's experience is too painful to be stored unchanged, or if such traumatic experience is denied or dismissed by parents, caretakers, or other significant adults in a child's life, this child may develop two conflicting internal models as a strategy to integrate the traumatic event (Colin, 1996b).

Continuity of Attachment

According to Bowlby (1973), attachment characterizes behavior from cradle to grave. By age three, most children show attachment behaviors less frequently than younger ones. Although frequency and attachment figure may change slightly at different developmental ages, its basic characteristics and patterns show marked continuity (Ainsworth, 1984, 1991).

A few longitudinal studies have been conducted over the past 20 years, mostly in California and northern Germany, to assess the stability of attachment styles across the life span. Patterns of attachment seem to remain stable throughout the life span. However, negative life events (such as loss of attachment figures due to divorce, illness, or death; parental substance abuse; child abuse and neglect; and changes in one's financial situation), seem to play an important role in the development of avoidant or anxious-ambivalent traits in adults classified as secure during childhood. In the absence of such events or significant changes, however, people's attachment styles seem to remain stable across the life span (Ainsworth, 1984).

One of the most dramatic periods of social development and change occurs during adolescence, and the attachment of a child to his or her parent changes greatly during that period. Other adults, institutions such as school and work, religion, sexual partners, and friends all can potentially become objects of attachment. During adolescence and adulthood the attachment to parents is usually weakened, as other figures replace some aspects of the parent's function and role. However, both extremes can also be found. Some individuals never "leave home" or develop emotional bonds to others, whereas others become almost estranged from their parents. "As a result, individual's variation, already great, becomes even greater." (Bowlby, 1982, p. 207). These increased variations have contributed to the less defined patterns, and the somewhat still vague field of attachment in adults.

Attachment and Psychopathology

According to Bowlby, most psychopathology can be traced back to separation and inadequate care in childhood. "Prolonged breaks in the mother-child relationship during the first three years of life appears to leave a characteristic impression on the child's personality. Clinically, such children appear withdrawn and isolated" (Bowlby, 1973, p. 32). Bowlby observed that many children who were separated from their mothers between the ages of 6 months and 3 years presented symptoms of anaclytic depression (2) and withdrawal; inability to form warm object relations; poor impulse control; regression in their development; and distortion in ego development. But as children got older, these negative effects were progressively minimized, as they continuously attained more solid object relations, were less dependent on care for survival, and developed a better sense of reality. (Bowlby, 1973). However, early "... separation from parents does not *necessarily* [italics added] lead to specific effects upon personality in later life, and . . . these personality patterns, when they are observed, are not *always* [italics added] due to a particular set of early experiences" (Bowlby 1973, p. 205). Physical and/or emotional separation from the mother will affect the child in different degrees, depending on (1) the quality or existence of alternative adequate care, before, during, and after the separation; (2) the stage of development of the child; and (3) the quality of later affectional bonds and life experiences.

The relationship between attachment and psychopathology has been investigated quite intensely in the past 20 years. Insecure attachment is not in itself a sign or symptom of mental illness, but it does seem to correlate and to be a risk factor for the development of psychopathology. Suicide, depression, substance abuse, conduct disorder, and most of the personality disorders, for example, seem to relate to early negative experiences and separation from the attachment figure, specially when paired with the unavailability of an adequate substitute attachment.

Insecurely attached individuals are more likely to see themselves as not worthy of love and nurturance, and to see others as unable to fulfill those needs. This internal working model of self and others can lead to depression and anxiety (Adam, 1982; 1994; Brennan & Shaver, 1995; Brown, 1982; Harris & Bifulco, 1991); higher rates of substance abuse (Kirkpatrick & Hazan, 1994); conduct disorder (Bates & Bayles, 1988); and to a pattern of forming conflictual and unfulfilled relationships in adulthood (Hazan & Shaver, 1987/ 1990; Kobak & Hazan, 1991; Shaver & Brennan, 1992).

The field of child psychopathology usually classifies symptoms in two broad categories: "Externalizing, with excess in aggression and exploitation, and internalizing, with excess negative emotion, inhibition, and avoidance" (Bates & Bayles, 1988, p. 255). Several studies suggest a correlation between attachment styles and particular predisposition in children and adolescents to develop internalizing or externalizing psychopathology. In a study with 60 adolescents admitted to a psychiatric hospital, Rosenstein and Horowitz (1996) found that a strong association between adolescents classified as dismissing and diagnosed as having conduct disorders, whereas those classified as preoccupied were more likely to present symptoms of affective disorders, such as depression and anxiety. Adolescents with a substance abuse diagnosis were twice as likely to have a dismissing organization of attachment. Finally, there was a significant correlation between attachment style and gender, with males more likely to be classified as dismissing, and females more likely to have a preoccupied organization of attachment.

Attachment, Loss, Depression and Suicide:
Parental loss, especially in the first 16 years of a person's life seems to represent a risk factor for depression. In an extensive literature review, Brown (1982) found a strong correlation between loss of the mother before the age of 17 and the onset of depression in adulthood. The loss of the father, however, did not seem to represent a significant contributor for pathology in adulthood. Bereavement in childhood due

to loss of the mother was associated with increased risk of suicide, severe depression, and anxious attachment in adulthood (Bowlby, 1980). In a study done in Scotland with over 5,000 psychiatric patients and 3,000 matched controls, Birtchnell found a significant increase in the incidence of depression in males and females who lost a parent, and in particular, the mother, before age 10. In addition, there was a higher incidence of alcoholism among females in the experimental group (Bowlby, 1980). Studies that defined loss not only by death, but that included desertion by the mother or father, and separation from the mother or father for one year or longer before age 17, also found a significantly higher incidence of depression in the experimental groups compared to controls. Although the literature is consistent in finding the loss of the mother before age 17 as strongly correlating to psychopathology, the loss of the father in childhood, although significant, seems to present a less strong correlation to the development of mental illness.

Careful analysis of earlier studies, however, point to the lack of control of variables such as the nature and quality of parenting before the loss occurred, or the quality of care after the loss. After reviewing over 60 studies, Parker concluded that it remains uncertain whether loss in itself predisposes "the child to depression in adulthood [or whether] any ill effects that follow may be more closely related to inadequate parental care preceding or subsequent to the loss or the loss itself." (Parker, 1994, p. 301).

Kenneth Adam studied and reviewed studies that investigated the correlation between early parental loss and later suicidal attempts and ideation. The incidence of loss among suicide attemptors seems to be between 32 and 42 percent higher (for repeated attempts) compared to non-suicidal controls, with loss of the parent between the ages of 10 to 14 being the most prominent characteristic among repeated suicide attemptors. Parental loss before age 14 constitutes a predisposing factor, which, when put together with precipitating factors (such as a recent loss or separation), and contributing factors (such as intoxication by alcohol or drugs, brain damage, or serious personality disorders), can lead to suicide attempts and completion (Adam, 1982).

The stages of mourning following the loss of the attachment figure are often used in a liberal way, to include not only the loss of the parent due to death, but also other forms of loss, such as prolonged separation and even chronic unavailability of the parent to the child. When classifying these stages, for example, Bowlby observed that children deprived from the company of the attachment figure due to lengthy hospital stays also experienced stages of mourning. According to Bowlby (1980), the process of mourning follows four distinct and predictable phases:

1. Numbing lasts between a few hours and a week following the loss of a significant attachment figure, and is characterized by intense distress and/ or anger.

2. Yearning and searching for the lost person lasts some months, and sometimes years. In this stage, the individual might in a moment of distraction, "forget" that the attachment figure is permanently unavailable (such as in the event of death), and may have fleeing thoughts or illusions of that person arriving home, for example, when hearing a familiar noise.

3. Disorganization and despair. During this phase, attempts to resume previous activities result in disappointment, frustration, feelings of emptiness, and lack of motivation.

4. Reorganization. This stage varies, depending on individual differences. During this stage, the mourning person starts to integrate the new reality with some success and with a feeling of some ease and satisfaction with daily activities.

Attachment and Disorders of Behavior and Conduct:
The relationship between attachment and conduct disorders has been studied extensively in children and adolescents. Young children identified with insecure working models of attachment are more likely to externalize their anger and frustration, presenting symptoms of conduct disorder and defiant behavior. Greenberg and Speltz (1988) concluded that such behaviors may be merely the result of the child's attempt to gain attention from an unresponsive caregiver. Bates and Bayles (1988) suggested that problems of behavior in anxious-ambivalent children may reflect their frustration with the concurrent emotional dependency of the caregiver and their inability to deal with

the high levels of anxiety they experience in the relationship. These children then express their ambivalence through aggressiveness and violence towards the attachment figure. Finally, avoidance may result from intense feelings of anger and frustration towards the attachment figure, which represents the main provider for the child. As the children realize their dependency on the caregiver for survival, they use avoidance as an adaptive strategy to keep their emotional integrity.

Intergenerational Patterns of Attachment

Researchers have studied attachment across generations and have consistently found that insecurely-attached mothers are more likely to have insecurely-attached children, whereas children of secure mothers are more likely to be securely-attached, creating what is known as intergenerational patterns of attachment (Van-Ijzendoorn, 1992; Van-Ijzendoorn et al., 1995; Van-Ijzendoorn & Bakermans-Kranenburg, 1997). Despite the limited number of studies and sample sizes, the correlation of attachment styles between parent, child, and in some studies, also grandparent, is impressive. In some studies, such correlation is 80% or higher.

Although little is known "about the mechanism of intergenerational transmission of parenting" (Van Ijzendoorn, 1992, p. 95), it seems that the working models of the attachment figure play a significant role in the quality of parenting (Das Eiden, Teti & Corns, 1995). This is one way to explain how attachment is passed on to future generations. However, here one should make the distinction between the parents' early attachment experiences and their current representation of attachment. What will influence their parenting style, according to attachment theory, is not their early experiences with their attachment figure, but rather how they integrate such experience cognitively and emotionally later in life. How, in adulthood, people explain the motives for the parents' actions and behavior, how they remember the parents' emotional availability, and how they put their childhood in context, all greatly influence how those adults will later make sense of the quality of parenting they received as children. These subtle differences may help explain how intergenerational patterns of attachment are not only formed, but most importantly, how they can be "broken". Finally, two other variables seem to be significant in a child's formation of a particular attachment style: social context, and the child's individual characteristics (Van Ijzendoorn, 1997). What remains to be determined is to what degree, and with what frequency, each of these variables is activated and how their interaction may influence the attachment style of the next generations.

Assessing Attachment Style

One of the first and most researched instruments for assessing attachment in adults is the Adult Attachment Interview (AAI), a semi-structured instrument developed by George, Kaplan, and Main, in 1984. It has 15 structured questions centered on the participants' recollections of their childhood and current relationship with the attachment figure. The interviewer asks the participants to choose five adjectives to describe the relationship with each parent or identified attachment figures during childhood, to describe particular events and behaviors, such as what they did when afraid or upset, as well as the characteristics of their current relationship with each parent. The transcribed responses are then systematically coded. Contradictions and inconsistencies, difficulty to easily access detailed memory of childhood events, intrusive thoughts, and "slips of the tongue", all are relevant to the coding system and the classification of attachment.

According to the AAI, there are four possible classifications of the adult's state of mind in relation to attachment: secure, dismissing, preoccupied, and unresolved (Colin, 1996b; George, Kaplan, & Main, 1996). This classification somewhat parallels Ainsworth's classifications of children as secure, avoidant, resistant, and Main's fourth classification of children as disorganized-disoriented. During the interview, secure adults are more likely to easily access and integrate positive and negative childhood experiences; they do not idealize their parents and are able to forgive the parents for past or present disappointments, conflict, and maltreatment. They also balance their need for the attachment figure with their need for independence and "exploration". Dismissing adults tend to report contradictory experiences with the attachment figure while at the same time they tend to idealize their childhood and parents, describing them as wonderful and flawless. They also tend to minimize their needs for a relationship with the attachment figure and have much difficulty remembering specific events from childhood. Adults classified as preoccupied seem to still depend emotionally on the parents and constantly seek their approval. Their stories are characteristically disorganized, tangential, colored by irrelevant descriptions, incoherence, and generalized or nonsense words and sentences, such as "bla-bla-bla," or "and all that". Unresolved adults tend to have a history of neglect, losses, trauma, or abuse in childhood. Their report of such experiences is often incoherent, oscillating between positive and negative views, and characterized by irrational interpretations for those events. (Colin, 1996b; George, Kaplan, & Main, 1996).

Several very large studies have been conducted to determine the validity and reliability of the Adult Attachment Interview, (or AAI) (Colin, 1996b; de Hass, Bakerman-Kranenburg, & van Izendoorn, 1994; van Izendoorn & Bakerman-Kranenburg, 1997), its validity across cultures (Grossmann & Grossmann, 1990), and its stability of classification within individuals (Benoit & Parker, 1994). There is sizeable evidence that, administered by trained persons, the AAI has high and consistent validity, reliability, and stability.

A much less complex tool to classify adolescent and adult attachment styles, the Attachment Style Checklist, was developed by Hazan and Shaver in 1987. It basically consists of three statements about how a person feels in close relationships, and each of those statements was designed to include the general characteristics of attachment as proposed by Ainsworth in her classification of children. Hazan and Shaver conducted large surveys using this instrument and found significant correlation between the attachment classification and (1) the respondents' reported relationships with their work and religion; (2) traits that placed them at risk to develop emotional problems; and (3) their reported satisfaction with partners (Hazan & Shaver, 1987; Hazan & Shaver, 1990; Kirkpatrick & Shaver, 1992; Kirkpatrick & Hazan, 1994; Kobak & Shaver, 1991).

Although several other instruments are available to classify attachment styles, discussion of those is beyond the scope of this project, since the two instruments mentioned are the ones I relied as part of the design of this project. The AAI was used as a departure point in designing the interviews for this study because it shared many characteristics with the qualitative method of data analysis and data collection. The Attachment Style Checklist, on the other hand, was useful in providing complimentary data relevant for this project, as it relates specific attachment styles to satisfaction in close relationships. In addition, the questionnaire was simple and quick to administer, and it would not represent an undue burden for the participants to respond or for this researcher to collect and analyze the data, even if later in the project it proved to be dispensable information.

ADOLESCENCE

Adolescence is a rich, complex, and challenging period in an individual's life. From the age of 13 to early adulthood, most people go through a period of introspection alternating with their attempts to explore the outside world. Many adolescents at times feel frustrated and angry about family rules they see as too restrictive, but also insecure and lonely as they doubt their ability to successfully negotiate the larger world. Finally, during these years, most individuals start the lifelong process of making choices in an attempt to comply with the demands of the outside world, and at the same time fulfill the inner needs and desires of the self.

Normal Adolescent Development

The developmental models of identity formation proposed by Erik Erickson, Peter Blos, Lawrence Kohlberg, Jane Loevinger, and Robert Keagan conceptualize, from different angles, the changes that occur in adolescence. Whereas non-developmental theorists see maturation and change as the unfolding of character traits that reside within the person and that are activated by experience, developmental theorists share the premise that changes and maturation occur in a stage-like fashion. Although somewhat predictable and organized within a particular structure, those stages are not necessarily linear (Kroger, 1996).

According to the developmental model, different stages of development are qualitatively distinct, and once such reorganization occurs, "... it is simply not possible to go back to view the world through earlier, less complex models of organization" (Kroeger, 1996, p. 7). Another common factor among the developmental theorists is the view that the intra-psychic balancing act of defining the boundaries between self and others has unique characteristics at each developmental stage and, during adolescence, this process is at its height.

The work of Blos (1962, 1967), with its grounding in object relations theory seems particularly relevant to be presented here, given some of its shared concepts with attachment theory. Put very succinctly, object relations theory proposes that in relationships, people react and interact not only with the actual individual before them, but also to the internal representation of others that originated from their early experience with the main caretaker. Therefore, I will focus on adolescent developmental stages and tasks according to the work of Blos because it seems to represent a relevant lens from which to look at the phenomenon of maturation during adolescence for the purposes of this study. Blos divided normal adolescent development into six distinct phases: The latency period, preadolescence, early adolescence, adolescence proper, late adolescence, and post-adolescence.

Latency Period:

Latency period is defined as the phase when the "dependency on parental assurance for feelings of worth and mastery are significantly and progressively replaced ... by a sense of self-esteem derived from achievement and mastery which earn objective and social approbation" (Blos, 1962, p. 54). During this period, ego functions, such as learning, memory, perception, and thinking become consolidated and instinctual functions do not threaten the ego as much as they did in earlier years. Increased social awareness and a better understanding of reality versus fantasy are also characteristic of this phase.

Preadolescence:

During this phase, according to Blos (1962), drive and competition increases. However, sexual drives are not yet well understood or integrated, leading to hostile interactions especially among boys towards the opposite gender. Such increase in drive can also be seen through the increase in acting-out and hostile behaviors characteristic of this phase. On the other hand, the child develops interests and skills that carry same-sex peer approval and prestige. There is mostly a quantitative increase in drive compared to a qualitative difference in drive that can be observed at the subsequent stage of early adolescence.

Early Adolescence:

During this stage, a profound reorganization of emotional life takes place. More than ever before, individuals are able to use the "emotional communication of others to guide their actions" (Gemelli, 1996, p. 465). At this stage adolescents are able to use empathy to relate and understand others. This empathic ability and the cognitive advances observed during this stage enables adolescents to "generate different hypotheses in planning their future [and] enables them to anticipate the feelings they assume will accompany each of their possible future choices" (Gemelli, 1996, p. 466). By early adolescence, values and beliefs are quite independent from parental influence.

During early adolescence, boys and girls substitute the image of the idealized parent with the newly developed image of the idealized, same-sex friend. In the typical early adolescence friendship, according to Blos (1962), idealization and eroticism blend in a unique way. In girls, "friendships, crushes, fantasy life, intellectual interests, athletic activities, and preoccupation with grooming in general protects the girls against precocious sexual activity." (Blos, 1962, p. 87).

Adolescence Proper:

This phase is characterized by the awakening of interest towards the opposite sex as the new attachment figure (or love object), and the break away from the parent as the main attachment or love object. The parent now is undervalued and the new love object takes on the role of being overvalued and idealized. The function of this shift in love-object is the beginning of the process of individuation and emotional separation from the parents. During this phase, a narcissistic and over-inflated sense of self-importance is also often seen in adolescents. This inflated sense of self helps the adolescent in his or her process of separation from the sense of the parent as a symbol of strength and protection. It is as if the adolescent has to feel overly capable and skilled to have the courage to start the process of separation from the family of origin. This unrealistic appraisal of one's abilities and skills will hopefully yield a more realistic self-appraisal once the adolescent enters the stage of late adolescence and feels better able to cope with the outside world (Blos, 1962; Gemelli, 1996).

Late Adolescence:

During this stage, the individual is increasingly able to act in a purposeful and planned manner, attains constancy of emotions, and a more stable self-esteem. The ability of adolescents to relate in the social world effectively also increases dramatically. Blos considers late adolescence as a stage of consolidation of the gains attained in the earlier stages, particularly the consolidation of a stable and integrated sense of self, regulation of emotions, and an irreversible sexual identity (Blos, 1962). During this stage, the decrease in the inflated sense of self and narcissistic qualities seen during the earlier phases will hopefully give place to a more realistic view of the self and of attainable goals for the future. The accomplishment of four main tasks characterize the closing of this phase: Establishment of autonomy from parents, establishment of realistic goals and realistic self-image, establishment of a stable sexual identity, and establishment of the ability for a stable mechanism of emotional regulation (Gemelli, 1996).

Postadolescence:

According to Blos, the final phase of transition into adulthood can be conceptualized as belonging to either one of the two developmental stages: adolescence or young adulthood. The main task of this phase is the integration and harmonization of the different aspects of one's personality. This integration "goes hand-in-hand with the activation of social roles, courtship, marriage, and parenthood. The appearance, or the manifest role of the young adult – having a job, preparing for a career, being married, or having a child – easily blurs the incompleteness of personality formation" (Blos, 1962, p. 149). In other words, although the individual increasingly assumes the external responsibilities and functions of adulthood, the development of one's personality and process of maturation is continuously unfolding.

Main Tasks During Adolescence

One of the main tasks during adolescence is the process of separation and individuation of the individual from his or her parents. The most important aspect of this process occurs at the emotional level: The emotional process of individuation is more crucial during adolescence compared to the physical separation from the parents. Although other theorists have talked about the process of individuation, I will again draw on Blos's (1962) concepts because they seem the most relevant frameworks to use for the purposes of this project.

<u>Blos's Theory:</u>
According to Blos, the four challenges of adolescence are "(1) the second individuation process, (2) reworking of childhood trauma, (3) ego continuity, and (4) sexual identity" (Kroeger, 1996, p. 49). Of those four tasks, the second individuation process has received the most theoretical, clinical, and empirical interest. Blos departs from Margaret Mahler's theory of infant separation-individuation as the basis for his proposition. According to Mahler, the infant begins life without an internalized representation of self or reality. During the first 8 weeks of life, the baby is in a symbiotic state with the mother, and during this normal *autistic* stage the infant's main goal is to maintain physiological homeostasis. By 10 months, the toddler can differentiate between self and mother, but it is only between the 15th to and the 22nd months that children are actually able to conceptualize themselves and their mothers as two distinct and separate psychological entities. By the third year, two main tasks should have been accomplished: the achievement of the basis for a life-long sense of individuality, and the attainment of object constancy. Object constancy can be defined as the child's capacity to internalize the "good" and the "bad" images of the mother and to start understanding that these two extremes are in fact part of the same reality (Kroeger, 1992, 1996; Mahler et al., 1975). In other words, the same responsive and nurturing mother may at times go through brief periods when she neglects our needs and desires. Blos proposed that adolescents go through a process of individuation that mirrors the earlier process of separation. He called this stage "second individuation".

Second individuation: The individuation processes observed in early childhood and in adolescence share common characteristics. "Both periods have in common a heightened vulnerability of personality organization, . . . the urgency for changes in psychic structure in consonance with the maturational forward surge, . . . and both periods, should they miscarry–are followed by a specific deviant development (psychopathology) that embodies the respective failures of individuation" (Blos, 1967, p. 163). Like the infant who must "hatch the symbiotic membrane," the adolescent must shed the dependency from the parents. This disengagement from the internalized parental representation will allow the adolescent to form extra-familial romantic attachments. Blos proposed that, whereas the task of individuation in childhood is to separate from the caretaker by internalizing its image, the psychological task of second individuation in adolescence is to disengage from this very internalized object (Kroeger, 1992, 1996).

As a result of successful individuation, the adolescent is able to attain a stable sense of boundary of self and others and to depend more on internal resources for self-regulation. This decreased dependency on external or parental sources of support will result in greater constancy of mood and self-esteem. Paradoxically, however, it is only through regression and the revisiting of unresolved infantile drives that adolescents can successfully complete the process of individuation (Kroeger, 1996).

Blos proposes that much of the usual behaviors of adolescence can be interpreted as regression to early childhood. The return to action rather than verbal language to express needs; the idealization of pop-stars as substitutes for the child's idealization of the parents; emotional states similar to merger (illustrated by the tendency to over-identify with certain political groups and beliefs); and the engagement in frantic activity to compensate for the sense of emptiness from object loss, all have parallels to earlier developmental stages. Blos also suggests that it is now the peer group who will provide the necessary support that will help adolescents cope with the pain of the object loss and the mourning over the loss of the childhood self (Kroeger, 1996).

Blos states that the attempt of some adolescents to disengage from their families by distancing themselves geographically, physically, morally, or ideologically, in fact arrests the process of psychological maturation. In fact, separating from "internal objects except by detachment, rejection, and debasement is subjectively experienced as a sense of alienation" (Blos, 1967, p. 168.).

Reworking and mastering childhood trauma: Blos argues that regardless of how kind and uneventful one's childhood, there are numerous opportunities for emotional injury, and mastering its effect is a lifelong project. During adolescence, much of this task is being accomplished, not through removal, but rather by integrating those events into one's character. By the closing of a "successful" adolescence, we will have remolded much of our childhood trauma into a mature ego organization (Kroeger, 1996).

Ego continuity: According to Blos, this is a third condition for character formation in adolescence. By the end of adolescence, the ability to "form one's own view of the past, present, and future emerges" (in Kroeger, 1996), and in situations where the individual must accept a distorted reality or deny one's own past to ensure survival, psychopathology is more likely to occur. For adolescents struggling to adapt to a new culture and family, and faced often with overt and covert racism and discrimination, this could be an additional challenge that places them at greater risk for unmanageable stress and mental illness.

Sexual identity: Blos argues that the only way for an individual to establish his or her sexual identity is by regressing to Oedipal conflict and resolving it, so that mature object relations can be initiated with others outside the family (Blos, 1967; Kroeger, 1996).

Blos's last three dimensions of character formation have received far less attention of theorists and researchers compared to the dimension of second individuation. Although his proposition that regression to earlier stages is a factual and necessary occurrence has received some empirical validation from longitudinal studies and clinical observation, his theory has certainly faced opposition and criticism. Some researchers argue that the constructs of differentiation and individuation do not lend themselves easily to assessment and measurement. Other researchers observe that turmoil in adolescence seems to indicate the presence of psychopathology, and that among "normal" adolescents, this stage of maturation evolves slowly and unremarkably. Finally, some of the literature points out that the releasing oneself from family dependency does not seem to necessarily apply to the maturation process of women, as women seem to mature within family relationships rather than out of them (in Kroeger, 1996).

Blos does not address specific cultural issues in adolescent individuation, but he does recognize the role of environment in that process. He states that no adolescent "can develop optimally without societal structures standing ready to receive him, offering him that authentic credibility with which he can identify or polarize. [In addition] . . . the psychic structure of the individual is critically affected, for better or worse, by the structure of society" (Blos, 1971, p.

975). Issues of culture and adolescence will be further explored later in this chapter

Creativity During Adolescence

There is a widespread notion that creativity and adolescence is linked. We all have noticed how during adolescence, most individuals become suddenly interested and involved in creative work, be it the performing arts, music, the fine arts, or writing rhymes and poetry (Cooper, 1990). Blos argues that introspection is at its height during adolescence, and that fantasy and creativity plays an important role in the expression of self during this stage of turmoil, but also of rapid and exciting growth and insight (Linesch, 1988).

> The heightened introspection or psychological closeness to internal processes in conjunction with a distance from the outer objects allow the adolescent a freedom of experience and an access to his feelings which promote a state of delicate sensitivity and perceptiveness. Adolescent artistic productions are often undisguisedly autobiographical and reach their height during the phases of libidinal withdrawn from the object world . . . The creative productivity thus represents an effort to accomplish urgent tasks of internal transformations. Blos, 1962, p. 125.

According to Rothenberg (1990), although creativity in the visual arts seems to decline during this period, poetry writing, music, and the less formal artistic productions such as Graffiti seem to "help solve and crystallize issues of identity ... in the adolescent phase" (Rothenberg, 1990, p. 420). Heightened anxiety about the future, mourning over the loss of childhood, and uncertainty about the changing nature of the relationship with parents all play an important role in this process. Feelings of isolation, loneliness, and a sense of being different and misunderstood may propel teenagers into trying to express themselves through the symbolic (and therefore, less threatening) medium of the arts. The idea of using a non-verbal form of data for this study was in great part related to the understanding that creativity and self-expression are congruent to the developmental stage of adolescence. I will now give the reader some background information on one form of art therapy often used in clinical practice known as *sandplay* or simply *sand therapy*.

Sandplay and Sand Therapy as Expression of Self:
The use of sandplay as a form of art and play therapy dates back to the early 1920s. It has its origins in psychoanalytic theory, and is akin to the concept of free association. Although it was originally used in play therapy with children, therapists now also use sand tray therapy in working with adults, couples and families.

> In sandplay, the adult plays as does the child, with seriousness. The playing aspect seems to provide access to an initiatory rite of entry for adults into feeling, affect, and the world of childhood. Lost memories are found again, repressed fantasies are released, and possibilities of reconciliation occur. Weinrib, 1983, p. 61.

In the U.S., the two major influences in the field of sandplay therapy are Dora Kalff, herself strongly influenced by Jungian concepts, and Margaret Lowenfeld, who, although also influenced by Jung, was mostly Freudian in her approach. Kalff believed that sandplay provides the opportunity for the many symbols to be channeled into a concentrated form of self-expression. Symbols are expressions of the inner and outer worlds, and they mediate and connect both individual and universal meaning (Kalff, 1980).

Historical perspective on sandplay therapy: In the 1920's, Margaret Lowenfeld, a pediatrician and child psychologist working at the Institute for Child Psychology in London, started using miniatures and a sandbox in the assessment and treatment of children under her care. She would invite the children to "build a world" using the many miniatures she collected by placing them in a small sandbox. Through this process, they had the opportunity to express and resolve inner feelings and conflict within a contained and safe environment, provided both by the physical limits of the sandbox itself, and the accepting and permissive environment provided by the therapeutic space. She called this technique the "Lowenfeld World Technique," and over the next decades her work became well known throughout Europe (Sjolund & Schaefer, 1994).

In 1933, the German child psychologist Charlotte Buhler developed a standardized method to differentiate and classify normal and pathological play, and other psychologists, such as Lucas Kamp and Erik Erickson studied the developmental aspects and gender differences in sandplay construction. However, it was not until the late 1940s that the use of sandplay as a standardized procedure and diagnostic tool was developed by Swedish psychologists Allis Danielson and Gosta Harding. They called it the Erica Method, named after the plant "Erica Telralix". "This plant is noted for its strengths and hardiness, and for its soft, pink, lovely flower" (Sjolund & Schaefer, 1994, p. 231). They implied that this assessment method combined elements of formal, structured observation with clinical intuition and the "softness and fragility of the empathic contact with the child" (Sjolund & Schaefer, 1994, p. 231). Although the Erica method of scoring is usually applied to children ages 3 to 12, some of its guidelines for observation can be applied to all age groups.

Empirical research on sandplay: Empirical research on sand tray use and sandplay therapy has mostly focused on three specific areas of study. Some researchers have been concerned with specific symbols and configurations of sand trays, others have researched the validity of sand tray technique itself, and a third group has focused on sand trays as an approach to identify specific populations (Rodgers-Mitchell & Friedman, 1994). Although few in numbers, the research studies done on the field of sand tray use as a therapeutic and research instrument are promising.

Research studies on the use of sand trays have included children, adults, and clinical populations as samples. In a study done with 74 college-educated adults, Denkers (1985) compared the Minnesota Multiphasic Personality Inventory (3) (MMPI) scores to characteristics of sand tray constructions and found significant correlation between specific patterns of sand trays and MMPI scales (Rodgers-Mitchell & Friedman, 1994). In another study done with 185 children ages 11 months to 18 years, Jones (1986) correlated the types of pictures produces in sand trays and developmental stages as proposed by Piaget.

In that study, specific patterns found in the sand tray constructions seemed to differentiate the children according to Piaget's five different stages of development (in Rodgers-Mitchell & Friedman, 1994). Finally, Kamp, Ambrosius & Zwaan (1986) used the sand tray configurations to distinguish between a psychiatric and non-psychiatric sample of children ages 10 to 11, and found significant differences in the patterns of construction among those two groups. Children in the non-clinical group used a wider range of categories and number of miniatures. They also seemed to use the miniatures in the sand tray to depict a static image. In contrast, those in the clinical group used fewer categories of miniatures, fewer number of miniatures, and moved the miniatures around both during the task and after the sand tray construction was completed (in Rodgers-Mitchell & Friedman, 1994).

General interpretation guidelines: No organized or official guidelines for understanding sand trays have yet been developed. Besides, there is a general resistance among researchers and clinicians to use sand trays as a diagnostic tool or to interpret sand trays using an overly restrictive and conclusive set of rules, particularly among Kalff's followers. Clinicians point to the dangers of trying to fit the analysis into a tightly fit mold, which could compromise the creative process and the individualized approach to interpretation of sand trays. They also argue that due to the large number of individual variables and possibilities, using statistical analysis has proven cumbersome. As a result, most interpretations of sand trays rely on clinical and qualitative accounts to establish patterns of construction and guidelines for interpretation. Therefore a more significant and relevant use of time and energy is to look at the sand trays as unique representations of the participants' experience, and to use their understanding and interpretation as the departing point from which to give meaning to their experience. However, using some general guidelines for observation can provide a template from which to begin the analytical and interpretative process.

In this study I used the technique of mapping, as conceptualized by Ryce-Menuhin, to look for patterns among the trays built by the participants, and to analyze and interpret their work. In addition, I also used the general principles proposed in the Erica Method of Assessment as a guide to interpret the participants' sand tray constructions. Please refer to the data analysis section, in Chapter 3, for

further discussion of the specific procedures I used for interpreting the
sand tray constructions.

LATINO ADOLESCENTS AND THEIR FAMILIES

Finally, the third conceptual framework that guided me in the design,
completion, and analysis of this study was that of cultural norms,
particular as they influence the concepts and expectations regarding
attachment patterns and the developmental stage of adolescence. I will
now briefly address some of the main points related to this issue that
seemed most relevant for this project.

Most characteristics of human attachment and adolescent
development are considered biologically based, and therefore are seen
as universal in essence. However, some of the particular expressions of
attachment styles and specific expectations and norms around
developmental stages during adolescence differ across cultures.
Therefore, such expressions and nuances are seen as environmentally
and culturally based.

Latino Cultural Norms and Families Relations

Latinos in general place high value on *familismo*, a sense of pride,
loyalty, and cohesion in the family. "It is a deep awareness of and pride
in family membership, which provides individuals with confidence,
security, and identity, and a well-integrated kinship system that is relied
upon heavily for support" (Freeberg & Stein, 1996, p. 458). The
concept of familismo applies not only to the immediate family, but also
to relatives. Family cohesion is often expressed by the expectation and
behavior of frequent exchange of goods, services, and support, and of
living in close proximity to one another.

When comparing 100 Mexican-American young adults to their
Anglo cohorts, researchers found a higher level of *familismo* and
collectivism towards parents in that first group. In addition, the
reported felt-obligation toward mothers was higher compared to
fathers. The construct "felt-obligation" among Mexican Americans
included behaviors such as avoiding conflict with parents, providing
assistance to them, and striving for auto-sufficiency (Freeberg & Stein,

1996). With exception of the wish for self-sufficiency, all the results above were consistent with those of previous research. Despite the wish for self-sufficiency be considered incongruent with traditional Latino values, this characteristic among this particular sample could be explained by the fact that the group studied consisted mostly of college students born in the U.S.. Therefore one could assume that this group comprised of fairly acculturated subjects (Freeberg & Stein, 1996). Keeping such differences in mind, one could assume that the principles of individuation and separation during adolescence among Latinos will take a slight different shape and norm compared to Anglo counterparts.

Attachment Across Cultures

Many characteristics of attachment styles and developmental stages seem to be biologically based, and therefore universal. However, the specific expression of attachment styles and adolescent behavior may vary depending on cultural, familial, and individual differences. Over the past two decades, there has been an increased interest around the issue of applicability of the tenets of attachment theory and developmental theory across cultures.

Studies on attachment have used mostly white subjects as sample, and have adopted almost exclusively the Western constructs of family structure, family relations, and of care-taking behaviors. One way to disentangle the issue of validity from the concepts of attachment across cultures is by differentiating the biological from the societal aspects of the attachment system (Main, 1990). Researchers and clinicians should be sensitive and knowledgeable about cultural values, and attentive to their influence on maternal behavior and mother-child interaction, since those elements will influence the classification of attachment styles. Studies in Germany, for example, found an over-representation of infants classified as insecure-avoidant (Grossmann et al., 1985) compared to normative samples in the U.S., and Japanese and Israeli children classified as anxious-ambivalent greatly exceeded the North American normative samples (Myake et al., 1985; Sagi et al., 1985)). Some of those differences and discrepancies in the prevalence of particular attachment styles seem to be explained partly by the different expectations and patterns of child rearing across cultures (Kurtz, 1992).

Attachment theory, as proposed by Bowlby, has been criticized as taking into consideration a single arrangement of child-mother relationship and childcare arrangement. According to Margaret Mead (1966), in the Middle East, for example, milk-ties, and not gestation, define the relationship between mother and child. In other words, the relationship between the child and the woman responsible for breast-feeding that child will influence the child's preferred attachment style. In China and India, multiple nurturing figures, from young girls to elders, are common in raising a child (Kurtz, 1992), and in Japan, discontinuity of style, from early indulgence to later strict discipline is the norm of child rearing. Among the Samoans, for example, mothers leave the young child in the care of other women as they go to work in the fields. Whether, despite these cultural differences, the three or four identified patterns of attachment in children and adults can still hold true across cultures remains to be determined.

Latino Values and Attachment

Parent's attitudes, beliefs, and values regarding children and child rearing have long been viewed as dictating child outcome. However, the complexity of the influences in a person's life, and the weak research results obtained thus far has caused a decrease of interest in this line of investigation (Arcia & Johnson, 1998). This was one of the reasons that I chose to use the qualitative method of research for this project. It seemed to me that the compartmentalized and reductionist approach intrinsic to the quantitative method of research was in part responsible for the inconclusive results. It also seemed more important to try obtain a more holistic understanding of the impact of parental influence in how children will later perceive the world rather than to look for statistical significance of each element in this complex and interactive process.

The traditional Anglo culture gives much value to personality traits associated with individualism, such as self-confidence and independence, whereas Latino culture is sociocentric, placing great importance in interpersonal obligation, respect for others, and personal dignity, usually expressed through proper demeanor (Harwood, 1992). In a two- part study, Harwood found, as expected, that Anglo and Latino mothers will try to socialize their children in accordance with those cultural norms. Traits that Latino mothers described as being desirable in their children included having respect for adults, being quiet, displaying appropriate social demeanor, and having behaviors that ensure proximity with the caretaker rather than engaging in active exploration. The Anglo mothers, in contrast, described as desirable the child traits of self-control, independence, and active exploration, whereas clingy and distressed infants were rated as least desirable. In the second part of the study, Harwood constructed vignettes describing different child responses, using plots used in the Strange Situation (4), and then asked mothers to interpret the child's behavior. Congruent with their stated values in the first part of the study, Anglo mothers focused on traits of personal competency, whereas Latinas focused on "maintaining proper demeanor in public context" (Harwood, 1992, p. 836). One could then speculate that whereas (psychologically well-adjusted) Anglo mothers would try to foster behaviors in their children that would facilitate the development of secure attachment, their Latino counterparts might foster insecure attachment behavior patterns in their children. From this perspective, Anglo mothers might show approval towards their children when they act in ways to increase their sense of independence from the family, whereas Latino mothers might reinforce behaviors that keep the child or adolescent close to the family of origin. For example, the expectation that children will leave the parents' home shortly after turning 18 is considered normative among Americans. Among Latinos, sons and daughters are expected to live in the parents' home until they get married, regardless of at what age that might occur.

Adolescent Identity Formation among Latinos

"The normative storms and stresses of adolescence are nowhere more evident than in the lives of adolescent immigrants in cultural transition" (Baptiste, Jr., 1990, p.4). For many of these adolescents, the balancing act of managing simultaneously their personal developmental task of separation-individuation from their parents and the transitional issues specific to immigration places them at increased risk for severe transitional conflict. One commonly reported cause of family conflict comes from the different rates of adjustment and acculturation among family members, as the children adopt American values and are able to function in the host culture much sooner than their parents. Secondly, they feel angry and confused by what they perceive as double standards in the parents' behavior. Parents resist their own acculturation and expect the children to remain loyal to the values of their original culture. At the same time, they also want the children to function as negotiators and liaisons with the outside world, and to make the best of the opportunities offered by American society (Baptiste Jr., 1990).

Feelings of anger and depression over the need to "start over" in the new culture seem to predispose immigrant adolescents for developing emotional problems. This is seen most often in adolescents who felt they did not have a voice in the parents' decision to immigrate (Baptiste Jr., 1990).

Latino Adolescents and Reunification Issues

In my experience working with immigrant adolescents I found many similarities to the process of adjustment as described by Baptiste. Immigrant adolescents reunited with their parents seem to experience a lack of voice over their destiny during two important events in their life. They feel powerless when the parents decide to leave them and come to the U.S. without discussing their decision with their family, without informing the children that they are leaving, and often times, without even saying goodbye to their children. Years later these children re-experience feelings of having no voice over their destiny when the parents tell them it is time to immigrate and reunite with their parents. Now the children are uprooted and separated from their surrogate parent to come to an unfamiliar culture and to join parents towards whom they feel little or no attachment.

In 1997, I was the clinical director of a school-based program that offered counseling and support for students identified as being in need of mental health services. That program offered a support group for Latino immigrant adolescents recently reunited to their parents in the U.S.. The group consisted of four Latino students, ages 15 to 19, who met for 8 sessions at their high school in the suburbs of Washington D.C. These adolescents discussed their experiences of separation and reunification with their parents in the U.S. At the end of the 8-week period, they reported that the adaptation to their parents and life in the U.S. seemed to go through 5 distinct stages. In the first few months, they said that nothing felt real or permanent (in fact, they named this first stage "floating in the air"). After that, there was a deep desire to return to their country, followed by a period of constant fighting with their parents. They said the fights were about everything and about nothing. These children started to spend a lot of time in their rooms, and withdrew emotionally. After a while, they started to build friendships and became more proficient in English and in functioning in the new culture. Finally, after about two years, most of them reported to start feeling good about being in the U.S. and considered staying here after graduation from high school. One cannot help but see the similarities reported among this group and Bowlby's stages of grief following the loss of the parental figure as described earlier in this chapter.

RELEVANT PREVIOUS RESEARCH

Studies on the issue of family separation due to immigration are basically non-existent. After extensive search, only a few relevant articles were found. A general report on the status of migrant West Indian children reunited to their parents in England after separation was included as a chapter of a book on Caribbean families (Arnold, 1996). Glasgow and Gouse-Sheese (1995) described the process of leading a support group in a Canadian school with Caribbean children reunited with their parents after prolonged separation. In a qualitative study with Central American children, Masser (1992) found separation from parents to be one of the three most important causes of trauma for those participating in the study. Finally, in a qualitative study with Central American domestic workers living in California, participants described how they gave meaning to their condition of *transnational motherhood*. Of those with children, a great majority had at least one child living with relatives or in other childcare arrangements in their country of origin (Hondagneu-Sotelo & Avila, 1997). Although there are numerous studies and reports on children in foster care, the very different cultural and familial context for those children makes it not relevant enough to be included in this project.

In an encompassing report on the status of Caribbean children reunited with their parents in England, Arnold (1997) described general attachment, parenting, and identity issues, as well as academic difficulties faced by these children. Reunited Caribbean children had difficulty identifying with their black heritage, and the social status of their parents, which was lower than they first perceived; they felt disoriented and confused about school expectations, and as a result, the majority of these students was identified as Educationally Subnormal (ESN). Many reported their frustration at the parental inability to accept their feelings of rejection, as the parents assumed that their children would feel happy upon the possibility of reunification and dismissed any feelings of grief over the loss of surrogated caretakers. Finally, parents had difficulty establishing bonds and closeness to the children who were left behind, as they experienced a closer and more rewarding relationship with the children they gave birth to after their arrival in England (Arnold, 1997).

Themes of rejection and abandonment were the most prominent for participants in a support group for Caribbean children reunited with their parents in Canada (Glasgow & Gouse-Sheese, 1995). The authors stated that separation and reunion seemed to be the main cause of difficulties in adjustment for those children and their families. Earlier reports and research on reunited Caribbean children concluded that depression and acting out behavior resulting from rupture of normal attachment due to separation from parents were the most common reasons for referral (in Glasgow & Gouse-Sheese, 1995). "Adolescents who felt abandoned had felt this way from the moment their parents departed. They did not accept the argument that parents left to make a better living for them abroad" (Glasgow & Gouse-Sheese, 1995, p. 6). These children reported that they felt reassured and loved when parents sent money and clothes and kept frequent contact with them. However, they also reported that, for the most part, their parents actually failed to do so. Other relevant issues brought up by the participants in the group were the loss of the surrogate caregiver after immigration and their disappointment over the quality of life in Canada. Parents often felt threatened if their children spoke of the caretaker during the separation, as if talking about that person meant the children were not grateful for the parents' sacrifice. During the visits of parents to their children during the years of separation, the children had a sense that the parents were rich and successful, as they often had good clothes and brought presents that often impressed the children. Once in Canada, they soon realized how little time parents had for family life, and how they struggled to make ends meet. Parents often expected the adolescents to contribute to the family finances, and these children often felt they were brought to Canada for the sole purpose of providing baby-sitting to the younger siblings and half-siblings. All this sounds painfully congruent with the reports I have often heard in working with reunited Central American children.

In contrast, in the research with Central American mothers who left their children behind, sacrifice was how most of the mothers participating in the study gave meaning to their decision to immigrate. Among this group, mothers, and not fathers, left their country because of the likelihood that they would be more successful in attaining work as housekeepers and babysitters once in California (Hondagneu-Sotelo & Avila, 1997). The authors point out that whereas upper-middle-class women have traditionally relied upon paid workers to care for their children (such as maids and nannies), lower class women have historically relied upon kinship for child care. For the women who had to rely on paid care while they sought work in the U.S., anxiety and fear that the children were being neglect or abused were a constant concern. Although all of the women participating in the study recognized that their primary role was to care for their children, circumstances pressured them to make cognitive and affective revisions to increase adaptability to their current reality. So they rationalized that sending money and other material things to their children was the best or only way they could care for their children at that time (Hondagneu-Sotelo & Avila, 1997).

Thirty-one Central American children seeking services in a health clinic in Los Angeles, California, were selected to participate in a qualitative study on trauma in children (Masser, 1992). Out of the 31, 25 had a history of separation from the parents, and in all cases the parents had immigrated first. Results indicated that a combination of stressors increased the probability of developing symptoms of trauma and meeting criteria for diagnosis of Posttraumatic Stress Disorder (PTSD) (American Psychiatric Association, 1994). The three strongest predictors of PTSD were if the child (1) had witnessed violence (war related, for the most part), (2) had been separated from the main caregiver, and (3) had other problems (mostly, if they lived in a stressful home environment due to poverty, family violence, or parental alcoholism). In this small sample, 100% met criteria for PTSD if the three conditions were present, but for those who did not experience caregiver disruption, only 50% met criteria for PTSD, even if they lived under stress at home and had been exposed to war trauma. In that study, the statistical analyzes of results is almost irrelevant due to the small size of the sample and the diversity of life conditions of these children. However, subjective observations validate the assumption that continuity of care is a very strong protective factor against PTSD in children exposed to traumatic events (Masser, 1992).

Implications for the Design of this Project

The literature on the topics of attachment, adolescence, and cultural norms among Latinos were the main guides in the design and implementation of this project. The small body of research on piecemeal immigration shed light and provided a preliminary map that organized my choices. The interview guide developed for this project was based on specific issues brought to light by the review of the literature on this topic and by my experience as a mental health professional. The interview guide questions were generally based on the premises of attachment in adults, the Adult Attachment Interview (George et al., 1996), on basic premises of adolescent development as proposed by Blos, and on relevant cultural issues of immigrant Latino families. The guidelines for the sand tray task as well as the parameters for analysis and interpretation of the sand tray constructions originated from the review of the literature on sandplay therapy as a clinical technique and research instrument. The knowledge obtained through the literature review was essential to direct the analysis and interpretation of data. Many of the coding categories that emerged during the process of analyzing the data reflected or confirmed some of the points brought up in the literature.

CHAPTER 3

Research Method Used

This study followed a topical design, focusing on the issue of separation from parents and the ways it affected the relationship with self and others, with the participants taking the role of experts. The data were generated from semi-structured interviews with each participant and from the construction of two sand trays: one sand tray at the end of each interview with every participant. Questions were particularizing rather than generalizing (Maxwell, 1996). This method was congruent with both clinical and interpretivist approaches. It was my hope that by the end of this project I would have gained a better understanding of how the perception and memories of separation were integrated in the participants' sense of self and how their sense of self shaped how they related to the outside world.

The influx of immigrants from Central America was caused especially by the outbreak of civil unrest and war in those countries for the past 20 years. The rapid growth of immigrant populations in large metropolitan areas, such as Washington D.C., has increasingly brought them to public attention. Among Central Americans, piecemeal immigration is a prevalent pattern, creating unique dynamics, needs, and consequences for these immigrant families and children. Despite its prevalence and importance, this issue has been virtually ignored by researchers.

The specific questions I intended to answer through this project were:

1. What meaning do young Central American immigrants who were separated from their parents in childhood give to that experience?

   a. How do they explain to themselves the parent's decision to immigrate and leave them behind?

   b. Is there a conflict between how they integrate the experience at the cognitive versus the emotional level?

   c. Is there a common meaning given by the participants to the experience of being left and to the decision made by the parent? If so, what are some of the salient cultural, community, familial, and individual characteristics?

2. What is the impact of separation on these participants' representational or internal working models of self? If there is indeed a dichotomy between conceptualizing the separation as *abandonment* versus *sacrifice*, what role does it play in the participants' internal working model of self?

3. What is the impact of separation on these participants' representational or internal working models of others?

   a. If there is indeed a dichotomy between conceptualizing the separation as *abandonment* versus *sacrifice*, what role does it play in the participants' internal working model of others?

   b. If there is indeed a dichotomy between conceptualizing the separation as *abandonment* versus *sacrifice*, what part does it play in the participants' current relationship with their parent(s)?

4. Does this life experience affect the emotional development of the participants? If so, how? What is the influence, if any, on how the experience is interpreted and integrated by the participants and the risk to develop psychological problems?

Due to the fluid and evolving nature of qualitative research, other themes, unexpected at the time I designed the project, started to emerge as I coded, analyzed, and interpreted the data. Those themes will be addressed in detail in chapters 5 and 6.

ASSUMPTIONS

It has been well documented in the literature, and it is my belief, that particular experiences in childhood and our perception about these experiences are key in determining how we will experience life and who we will become. The quality of the relationship between mother and child is essential in shaping people's sense of self, their ability to trust others, the quality of future relationships, and vulnerability to psychopathology (Ainsworth, 1984; Ainsworth, 1991; Bowlby, 1988).

Non-verbal expressions of self are helpful in illustrating core, undefended feelings, conflicts, and perceptions that individuals may have of themselves and of the outside world (Bowyer, 1970; Fisher, 1950). It was my hope that through sensitive interpretation of the participants' visual arts product (such as that provided by interpreting a sand tray construction), I would better understand how the participants integrated and gave meaning to the experience of separation and reunification. Including the sand tray task provided a wealth of non-verbal (and therefore, less intentional) data and information about the participants' feelings and internal states.

I also believe that preconscious and unconscious processes influence much of our choices. Although people build defenses and "blind spots" to decrease discomfort and pain they are not yet ready to face, a small window to the unconscious can be uncovered if we look beyond the surface. I believed that I would better understand how the participants in this study constructed and gave meaning to their experiences in dealing with reality if I focused on how they told their stories, the links they made through metaphors, the areas and topics they avoided, and how they handled symbolic material through art.

These assumptions were expressed in the choices I made during the course of this project. Therefore it was my responsibility to ensure that such assumptions provided me with a solid guide and framework to interpret the data without becoming a rigid fence around preconceived concepts and expectations.

ETHICAL ISSUES

Raw data were kept in a safe place accessible only to the researcher, and all identifiable information was altered to protect the anonymity of each participant in this and any future publication of this study.

Participants were informed that they could withdraw from the project at any time, with no penalty. Participants were also fully informed about potential risks of emotional distress caused by remembering or reporting on possibly painful life events. The participants' well-being was protected to the full of my ability. I tried to keep an empathic, yet professional demeanor; I was prepared to alter or terminate the interview should any participant become disturbed or too distressed during the interview; and I was also prepared to suggest and/or obtain immediate follow up assistance through referrals and/or follow-up contact. Finally, I made clear to all participants that they were welcomed to contact me at any time in the future, should they feel the need to obtain additional support, relief, or clarification regarding the content and processing of material elicited by the interview.

Whereas the goal of a therapeutic relationship is to decrease distress and correct or treat poor functioning, the goal of the interviewer in a research relationship is to learn from the perspective of the participant (Seidman, 1991). Therefore, every attempt was made to keep appropriate ethical boundaries and to avoid dual-role relationships during this project. There were no incidents that required intervention or referral to outside agencies during the data collection phase of this project.

All interviews were conducted by me. I am licensed as a professional counselor and marriage and family therapist, with extensive experience in assessing and dealing with persons under emotional distress. I am also knowledgeable of available community resources, and was prepared to make appropriate referrals or to intervene immediately, if needed. Therefore, should any problems arise, participants would have been properly assessed and dealt with in a professional and effective manner. Participants were not misinformed or uninformed about the true nature of the project, and there was no deception involved in this project.

DATA COLLECTION

Data were collected during the later part of the fall, 1999, and consisted of verbal accounts (interviews) and visual arts products (sand tray constructions). Participants were identified and referred by educators and mental health professionals I collaborated or worked with in the past. I did not have any prior contact with the participants, with the exception of two of the females interviewed. I was the clinical supervisor for the counselor providing therapy to one of the females 2 years before the interviews for this project took place. I also conducted a clinical assessment to another of the females participating in this project and referred her and her mother to one of the clinicians working in the agency I was employed at the time.

Interviews were conducted either after school or on weekends at a non-profit human services agency located in the suburbs of Washington, D.C. The art therapy room used for the interviews was private, quiet, and equipped with the sand tray and miniatures needed for this project. Participants described their experience of separation from and reunification with their parents during the semi-structured interviews, and then were asked to "build a world" by placing miniatures in a wooden box filled with sand (sand tray).

Screening Process

The meet criteria participants had to: (1) be between the ages of 14 and 19 at the time of interview; (2) have reunited to their parent or parents in the U.S. within the past 8 years; (3) have been separated from their biological mother, father, or both, for at least 3 years; (4) have the onset of separation between birth and the age of 12; and (5) be born in Central or South America. I also wanted to have similar number of males and females participating in this study. Finally, I hoped to have a sample of participants identified as being in need for mental health services and those not identified as having such need. All these objectives were achieved.

Participants were identified through word-of-mouth and through an informal network of mental health professionals and educators. These professionals helped me identify adolescents who met the criteria, and asked their permission to be contacted directly. I then contacted the prospective participants (and their parents, for those under 18 years old) and conducted a further telephone screening to ensure they would be appropriate to participate in this study.

During this first telephone contact, I briefly explained to the potential participants (and to their parents, it they were under 18), the purpose and nature of the project, and the procedures involved. I also asked specific questions to ensure that they met criteria to participate in this project (see criteria listed above). With no exception, all persons contacted seemed very pleased to be invited to the project and none of them refused to participate. Four prospective participants were excluded from this project because of being under the age of 14, for having a history of heavy drug use, or for being unavailable or very difficult to reach due to frequent incarceration at the local juvenile detention center.

The parents that I spoke with seemed very interested in the topic because they felt they could relate what I was describing to their own lives and experience of immigration. Some of them expressed interest in being interviewed and wished that their side of the story would also be heard. My response in those cases was that, although a very important aspect of this topic, it was beyond the proposed scope of this project. A few of these parents hoped that I would provide counseling to their families, that I would help them access community resources (such as housing and health care), or that I would be able to help them attain employment. In those cases, I provided the names and telephone numbers of social services agencies and counseling centers that might be helpful to them and again tried to explain the nature and reason for my contacting them. Nonetheless, their urge to talk to me seems to illustrate the level of need among these families as well as their lack of information on how to access available resources.

Sample

Four females and three males from Central and South America, ages 15 to 19, were interviewed. They arrived from Central and South America within the past 7 years (ranging between 2 and 7 years), after being separated from their mothers and/or fathers for at least 5 years, with the onset of the separation between birth and age 9. Participants were generally emotionally healthy, but two of them presented with some externalizing behaviors, such as defiant behaviors and conduct disorder. Three others had some internalizing behaviors, such as depression and anxiety. Psychotic, cognitively impaired, and heavy drug users were excluded from this project and fictitious names were used.

Table 1. Description of Participants

	Jorge	Suzana	Isabela	Rita	Luis	Carla	Alex
Age*	19	17	19	16	15	19	18
Country of origin	El Salvador	Colombia	El Salvador	El Salvador	El Salvador	El Salvador	Guatemala
Gender	Male	Female	Female	Female	Male	Female	Male
Age at separation from mother	9	1	9	7	6	6	2
Age at separation from father	8	Birth	15 by death of father	Birth	Birth	Birth	3 months
Age at reunification	16 (Mo. & Fa.)	10 (Mo.)	17 (Mo.)	14 (Mo.)	12 (Mo.)	16 (Mo.)	13 (Mo. & Fa.)
Length of separation-years	8 (Fa.) 6 (Mo.)	8 (Mo.)	8 (Mo.) 5 (Fa.)	7 (Mo.)	3 (Mo.)	10 (Mo.)	13 (Fa.) 11 (Mo)
Main caretaker during separation	Grand Parents	MGM	Boarding school and self	MGM, uncles, aunts	Maternal Grand mother	MGM & uncles	Maternal Grand mother
Marital status of Parents	Married	Never Married	Widowed	Never Married	Separated	Never married	Married
Birth order	Middle of 6	Only child	Oldest of 3	Oldest of 2	Youngest of 6	Oldest of 3	Youngest of 3
Grade at School	11	12	11	10	9	12	11

Procedures

In some cases I mailed a description of the project and the informed consent letter to the participants and their parents prior to the first interview. In other cases, I made sure to meet with the parents the day I picked up the participant for the first interview. That procedure seemed particularly important for the parents of the younger participants.

Transportation Issues:
After considering the advantages and disadvantages of picking up the children in their homes and driving them to the interview site, I decided that providing transportation to them was my best option. It guaranteed that the participants would be at the interview site and that they would be there on time. It also lessened the burden on the parents, for whom lack of transportation is often an issue. Finally, it provided the time and a relaxed environment to talk to the participants. I soon realized that I could use the car ride to describe exactly what the participant would encounter once we arrived at the office where the interviews would take place. I believe this strategy greatly helped to decrease their anxiety about meeting a stranger in a strange place. I often mixed "small talk" with relevant information about myself and general information about the nature of this project. For those who met me directly at the interview site, I noticed that it took them much longer to feel relaxed and comfortable with me and with the interview situation.

Stipend:
A small stipend was available to any participant willing to accept it, and upon parental approval for those under 18 years of age. The financial compensation for their time represented a concrete way to demonstrate my appreciation for the time and effort of each participant and allowed for reimbursement of any costs they might have incurred. This had mixed results. For most of the participants, the financial compensation seemed to be an initial incentive, but almost without exception, the participants wanted to decline being paid once the interviews were completed. There was some embarrassment on their part, greatly explained by cultural norms, but mostly, a sense that they benefited from telling me their stories and that the process itself was enough of a reward for them. Whenever I perceived their ambivalence or embarrassment about receiving monetary compensation, I made sure

to discuss the issue openly. Once I clarified that they were not being "paid" for their participation in the study they seemed more comfortable with the procedure. I also explained to them that if I knew them a little better, I would have preferred to give them a small gift, such as a book, a compact disk, or chocolates, and that I hoped that they would use the money to treat themselves to some small memento. By the end of our conversation, the participants seemed comfortable with the money issue. However, if I were to repeat this project today, I would give the participants a gift certificate to a bookstore or some other specialty retailer and avoid the direct monetary compensation altogether.

Interview Format and Guidelines

I met individually with each participant on two different occasions, and each interview was scheduled about one week apart. Each session began with a semi-structured interview that lasted about 90 minutes, followed by the sand tray task, which took about 15 minutes to complete. The interviews were audiotaped, and participants spoke in Spanish, English, and often, a combination of the two languages. The two-interview format seemed the most logical breakdown for the information I was seeking, as it matched the two-part data I intended to collect: the participants' memories about the period of separation from and reunification with their parents. By interviewing the participants on two occasions I also hoped to (1) have a chance to review and clarify topics and responses raised in the first meeting; (2) give all involved a chance to feel more comfortable with each other, increasing the probability of obtaining a true account of facts, feelings, and thoughts about their life history; and (3) make the length and frequency of the interviews comfortable and adequate for the participants and the interviewer.

At the beginning of the first interview I reviewed the purpose of the project, the plan for the day, confidentiality and other ethical issues, and answered any questions or concerns that the participants had. I also informed them that after the two face-to-face interviews were completed a follow up telephone contact might be necessary for clarification and additional questions. However, I found that such telephone follow up was not necessary.

Content of the Interviews:
The first interview focused on the participant's memories and impressions about the period of separation from their parents. The questions included some of the premises and general ideas included in the Adult Attachment Interview (George et al., 1996). For example, I asked the participants to give me two or three adjectives that best described the nature of their relationship with their mother and father prior to the separation, and their relationship to their main caretaker during the years they were apart from their parents. Parallel to the format used in the AAI, I then asked the participants to tell me some specific event that illustrated the adjectives they chose to describe those relationships (Please refer to Appendix A, "Interview Guide" for further details). In addition, I included in this first interview session specific questions about cultural issues that were relevant for this project. For example, I asked the participants about the family and community thoughts, interpretation, and justification for the parents' immigration and separation from their children.

At the beginning of the second interview I briefly reviewed the previous meeting and asked participants whether they had any thoughts or comments related to the first interview. To my surprise, many of these children seemed to have given some thought to the interview during the week. Some reported feeling a little sad about remembering their childhood, whereas others felt it was a relief to have the opportunity to talk about this topic to someone. In many cases, this was the first time they had such opportunity. None of them reported feeling distressed or overwhelmed after the interview.

The focus of the second interview was on the period and the process of immigration to the U.S. and reunification to their parents. I was interested in the participants' memories of those first months, the process of adjustment to American schools, the characteristics of their current relationship with their parents and significant others, and their overall goals for the future. I also asked the participants to respond to the Attachment Style Checklist by choosing 1 out of the 3 statements that they felt best described their relationships with others (Hazan & Shaver, 1987). Their choice could suggest their preferred attachment style in relating to others. Please refer to Appendix A for further information on the interview guide and the Attachment Style Checklist statements (Hazan & Shaver, 1987).

Sand Tray Activity Guidelines:
At the end of each interview, the participants engaged in an experiential activity where they were asked to "build a scene" or "build a world" by placing miniatures on a wooden box filled with sand (sand tray). The sand tray constructions were then photographed for future analysis and interpretation. I used the format and guidelines of sandplay therapy to guide the sand tray activity.

Sandplay therapy is done using a wooden box of standardized size (19.5"x 28.5" x 3"), with its bottom painted blue, so as to represent bodies of water. The sandbox is placed on a tray, about waist-high, and water is provided, should the participant prefer to use wet sand. The specific size of the box and its placement allows for the entire sand tray to be in one's visual frame all at once, which can facilitate the gestalt of the experience. Miniatures are arranged in an open shelf, divided by categories.

The basic categories provided were:

1. People and humanoid life forms, with family sets, naked figures, primitive and symbolic figures, such as queens, kings, religious figures, and half-human figures.
2. Animals, including wild and farm animals, insects, birds, and extinct or symbolic animals, such as dinosaurs and unicorns.
3. Plant life and minerals.
4. Environments, or structures, such as houses, bridges, lighthouses, and fences.
5. Transportation and communication miniatures, such as cars, boats, airplanes, and telephones.
6. Miscellaneous, to include the symbolic and magical items, such as treasure chest, coffins, cultural and religious symbols, sand tools, pieces of fabric, etc. (Please refer to Appendix A for details on instructions for the sand tray task as given to the participants).

DATA ANALYSIS

I used the interpretivist philosophical approach to analyze and interpret the data. According to this line of inquiry in qualitative research, what people report and how they act cannot be analyzed or fully understood through the traditional methods of research used in the natural and physical sciences. Interpretation of meaning is achieved through empathy and the repeated readings of interview transcripts, until the essence of the informant's account is finally understood (Brown et. al., 1988). An interpretive approach differs from coding in that it "demands attention to context-situational, personal, cultural, and therefore, to [the] perspective of both the participant and the researcher" (Brown et al., 1988, p. 2). Those characteristics made interpretivism an adequate approach to use, considering the unique and contextual circumstances of the separation due to the need to immigrate. In addition, this method was congruent with both the clinical tradition and the approach to research with minorities.

As a first step, I simply identified and coded the interview segments for particular themes and categories that might be relevant to answer my initial research questions. Later, I listened to all tapes two more times, in an effort to recapture the gestalt of the experience I had during the interviews. I made notes about my own reactions to the participants, including thoughts, feelings, associations, and intuitions I had: both, at the time of the interview, and as I later heard their stories on tape. This was the strategy I used to achieve empathy and to incorporate other elements of the interpretivist approach in my data analysis, including contextual-situational factors, cultural issues, and individual circumstances. This approach to data analysis also helped me find common patterns and threads among the participants and their stories. I predicted that the finding and reporting of repeated patterns and themes across participants would strengthen the validity and reliability of my interpretations, results, and conclusions.

Coding

The N-Vivo Nud*ist computer software (1999) was used to create codes and categories, identify segments that were relevant for analyses, organize memos, and for other data management tasks. Data were first coded following a topical design approach. Segments related to different topics, such as separation, family meaning to the departure of parent, quality of relationship with surrogated caretaker, quality of current relationship with significant others, clinical or personality traits, and attachment issues were identified and coded across participants. Patterns and some general themes then began to emerge, and new codes were created. A total of 30 coding categories (or nodes) were identified and created. Thirteen of them were categorized as "free nodes" - the term used by the N-Vivo Nud*ist software to represent categories that do not belong to a hierarchical format. These free nodes included categories such as school related issues, stories about war, traumatic events, losses, and career plans. Please refer to Table 2 below for a complete list of the free node categories.

In addition to the free nodes, three hierarchical categories with their respective subcategories were identified. Hierarchical categories are referred as "tree nodes" by the N-Vivo Nud*ist computer program. The tree nodes created were named "Damaged Goods", "Heroes", and "Love". Participants often described how the caretakers or parents loved them by talking about particular behaviors, such as cooking for them, sending money and presents, talking to them, playing, or punished them if they misbehaved. Therefore, it seemed to make sense to create a category called "Love", with subcategories that related to particular behaviors. "Heroes" included segments where the participants described the parents, themselves, their culture, or their family as doing something they were proud of or that exemplified their "specialness". On the other hand, "Damaged Goods" were segments identified as relevant because the participants described themselves, their families, culture, or their lives in negative or hopeless terms. Please refer to Table 2 for further information on the categories created for analyzing the interview transcripts.

Table 2. Coding Categories

FREE NODES	TREE NODES		
	DAMAGED GOODS	HEROES	LOVE
Abandonment	Culture as damaged	Culture as hero	Food

Career			Money
Competency	Parents as damaged	Parents as heroes	Playing
Divided Loyalties			Presents
Trauma	Self as damaged	Self as hero	Punishme nt
War			Talking
Sibling bonding	Life as damaged	Life as hero	Going out
Shame			Respect
School			Spoiled
Sacrifice			
Role Reversal			
Losses			
Guilt			

In addition to these "true categories", other nodes were identified mostly for easy recognition for further use, such as interesting quotes I might decide to use. Therefore, I also identified and coded segment as "good quotes", "sand tray talk", and "metaphors".

As I coded and analyzed the transcripts, I started formulating some hypothesis and identifying patterns across data and participants. I then identified segments that described critical incidents, i.e., incidents that represented turning points in the experience of the participants or in the way they gave meaning to their experience. In my work as a therapist working with children with a history of prolonged separation from their parents, for example, I often heard these children describe their longing for their surrogate caretakers when they were ill, or their disappointment over their parents' emotional distance when they felt sick or distressed. I pondered that such spontaneous reports might be relevant considering that attachment theory anticipates that people will seek proximity to the attachment figure in the event of threat or perceived threat (Bowlby, 1988). However, during the interviews for this research project, few participants actually brought up examples or stories related to longing for their mothers or caretakers in times of illness.

I looked for metaphors to understand individual and collective meaning of the participants' experiences. The significance of metaphors in discourse has been documented extensively in both clinical reports, and qualitative research. Metaphors include analogies, similes, and imagery. "At its simplest, a metaphor is a device of representation through which new meaning may be learned. At its simplest, metaphors illustrate the likeness (or unlikeness) of two terms (or linguistic framework)" (Coffey & Atkinson, 1996, p. 85). They give accounts that justify and evaluate actions taken, and can reveal shared social and cultural understanding of a situation or phenomenon. Therefore, metaphors could help reveal not only shared meaning of events or explanations of those events among the participants but, possibly, unforeseen links between events and their meaning.

Sand Tray Analysis

Two methods of sand tray analysis were used in this project: The Erica Method of Assessment (Sjolund & Schaefer, 1994), and Ryce-Menuhin's (1992) mapping approach to interpreting sand trays. In the Erica method, the analysis of the sand tray is divided into the formal aspect of the construction and into its content. The second method I used to interpret the sand trays was the Ryce-Menuhin (1992) "mapping" approach to interpret sand trays. However, instead of analyzing each sand tray using all the 8 maps, as proposed by Rice-Menuhin (1992), I chose to use only two of his proposed configurations. I will elaborate further on these two configurations in the next section of this chapter.

Erica Method of Assessment:
I used some of the basic principles used in the Erica Method of Assessment of sand trays to help me better understand internal conflict and processes of the participants of this project. Briefly described, the Erica Method of Assessment can be divided into two levels: the formal aspects of the construction, and analysis of the content. From those two elements, the clinician or researcher can formulate hypotheses about the sandplayer's developmental level, personality, strengths, defenses, and psychological problems.

Form was analyzed by looking at 6 basic elements:

1. The sandplayer's treatment of the sand: Was it gentle, repetitive, or inhibited? Was there evidence of poor impulse control? Did the participant hide objects?

2. The number of miniatures used: Did the participant use very few objects and categories? Were there too many objects? Were human figures absent? Were the miniatures chosen from a wide variety of categories? Whereas very few objects and categories may suggest the presence of depressive symptoms, the absence of human figures could indicate avoidant personality traits.

3. The developmental level of construction. Young children, for example, tend to use mostly exclusively plant life and animals, few miniatures, and categories, and will often hide objects in the sand or play in the sand rather than build a scene on it. Were scenes organized around themes? Did the placement of objects seem to be intentional and deliberate?

4. Changes and corrections. Frequent changes can indicate self-criticism, self-doubt, and anxiety. The order of the miniatures chosen is also important, as the first piece often will determine the "theme" of the scene.

5. The presence or absence of verbalization during the task, which could indicate level of discomfort or inability to get involved or invested in a loosely structured task.

6. Level of composition. This was further subdivided into configuration, simple categorization, juxtaposition, conventional grouping, meaningful scene, and atypical composition (Sjolund, & Schaefer, 1994). Such characteristics are assessed to determine the level of comfort subjects demonstrate in dealing with materials in a more abstract manner. Are miniatures used in a conventional grouping or is the participant comfortable in working creatively with what they represent? Do the miniatures share more than one characteristic?

I also analyzed the *content* of the themes illustrated by identifying its four main elements:

1. Predominant themes: Were they mostly violent, cooperative, concrete, or symbolic?

2. Sandplayer's approach to the task: Level of motivation, affect, decisiveness, etc.

3. Content of the verbalizations during the task: What was being said during and after the sand tray was completed? Were spontaneous stories or explanations provided? Were they coherent with the images being created?

4. Title chosen for the sand tray: Was the title creative? Humorous? Concrete? Literal?

<u>Sand Tray Mapping:</u>
I looked at the mapping of the trays following the guidelines proposed by Ryce-Menuhin (1992). After studying and comparing over 1,000 sand trays done by children, adolescents and adults, Ryce-Menuhin found that 95% of those trays followed eight specific patterns of design, so he mapped the trays following those patterns. Ryce-Menuhin argued that such maps are helpful in providing "hints and glimpses . . . of tendencies present in the sandplayer's psyche" (Ryce-Menuhin, 1992, p. 97). He classified the trays into 7 different levels, , using basically a combination of conscious, personal and collective unconscious (5). After analyzing all the sand trays using all the 8 maps (or figures), I found that some of the "maps" or "figures proved either unnecessary or vague to address the particular questions I had for this study. The interpretation of collective unconscious and archetypes, for example, fell into that category. Therefore, I chose to concentrate only on figures 3 and 8.

Figure 3 suggests that the sand tray should be divided horizontally into an upper and lower section. The upper part of the tray represents the conscious or more deliberate processes of the sandplayer's internal state and internal conflict whereas the lower part of the tray represents less deliberate processes. Therefore, if I were to compare the characteristics of the sand trays as divided in their upper and lower halves, I might find some relevant aspects about the participants' internal conflict. Figure 8 suggests that the clinician or researcher notice the center of the tray as a representation of the sandplayer's ego, or self. Consequently, I thought that this map configuration might be relevant in trying to find characteristics of the participants' ego strength. Please refer to Appendix C for examples of the types of maps commonly seen in sand trays and protocols for analysis.

Anticipated Results

From previous professional experience working with this population and the limited literature on the issue, I anticipated the following results:

A. Central American immigrant children separated from their parents would have ambivalent thoughts and feelings about the meaning of the parent's decision to leave them behind. On a cognitive level they may explain the parents' behavior as sacrifice, and still experience strong feelings of rejection and abandonment. Affect may be more clearly represented through the narrative and sand tray analysis compared to the more linear process of coding. Finally, congruent with cultural and familial values, those adolescents would probably explain the parent's behavior in consonance with the acceptable cultural and familial meaning given to that behavior. Even if participants were well defended against seeing the parent as abandoning, withholding, or rejecting of them, their internal conflict and the affective or individual perception of immigration as abandonment could become more evident in their non-verbal expression.

B. If there was indeed an internal struggle in conceptualizing the separation as *abandonment* versus *sacrifice*, that conflict would play an important role in the participants' internal working model of self and others. Participants who interpreted the parent's behavior as sacrifice (even if only at a cognitive level), might have been better equipped to face the challenges of individuation, adjustment, and acculturation. On the other hand, those who interpreted the parents' departure as rejection and abandonment (possibly due to their maturity level or personality style), were at a higher risk to internalize the experience as a direct assault on their sense of identity and self-worth.

C. Participants with a history of separation from parents would be prone to develop psychological problems. Furthermore, the way they would manifest those problems through symptoms might in fact correlate to their ability to integrate ambivalence. Those with a more immature and concrete psychological structure would be more likely to act out their difficulties, whereas the more psychologically mature and emotionally healthier participants would develop more internalized symptoms, such as depression and anxiety. However, I expected that most of the participants would report some symptoms of Posttraumatic Stress Disorder, whether they presented with externalizing or internalizing behaviors or symptoms.

I also expected that some themes would emerge from the data and across participants. The most important themes I anticipated included: (1) The participants' expressed desire and need to be in close proximity to the parent or the caretaker at times they fell sick; (2) Reported feelings of sadness, frustration, and anger as these children perceived their parents as unable to provide them with a sense of security and protection (a secure base) at times when they felt vulnerable; (3) Reported difficulty in trusting and communicating with others, especially with important people in their lives, such as their parents; (4) Seeing the parent's actions of sending money and presents during the period of separation as a symbol of these parents' concern, love, and ability to appropriately fulfill their role as parents.

Limitations of the Study

Issues of validity and generalizability are of concern in any research project. In qualitative research, the characteristics and definition of such terms take on a slightly different turn.

Validity Issues:
Validity refers to the concept that the descriptions, interpretations, conclusions, explanations, and theories generated from the data in a study are, in fact, an accurate representation of reality. This reality, however, depends on context. It is not the researcher's goal to imply "the existence of any objective truth to which an account can be compared... nor ...[is the researcher] required to attain the ultimate truth in order for [the] study to be useful and believable" (Maxwell, 1996, p. 87). This criterion is even more relevant to consider when working with culturally diverse participants. I describe here not an exhaustive list of possible threats to validity in qualitative research, but rather, the ones I saw as most relevant to this project and how I tried to address those threats.

One of the main threats to the validity of interpretive qualitative research is that researchers might impose their own "framework or meaning, rather than understand the perspective of the people they studied and the meaning they attached to their words and actions" (Maxwell, 1996, pp. 89, 90). This threat was minimized by (1) bracketing (or being explicit about) my own framework and assumptions, (2) presenting preliminary results to the participants during the follow-up telephone call for their feedback (member check), and (3) by asking open-ended, non-leading questions.

A second threat to validity in this study was participant's *reactivity*, or the influence of the researcher on the participants' accounts (Maxwell, 1996). I am a female Latina, and gender and cultural issues might have influenced the participants' responses. Hopefully, my professional training helped create a permissive and non-judgmental environment during the interviews, minimizing the danger of participants responding to their perception of the researcher's expectations or wishes. Whenever I got the sense that a participant was responding in any particular way to fulfill perceived expectations, I attempted to clarify the issue immediately and appropriately. For example, one of the participants (Alex) seemed uncomfortable with the idea that the research setting was somewhat similar to a psychotherapy session. Alex was particularly concerned that there may be anything "wrong" with him or his family. The message was subtle but important. So, I decided to bring it out in the open immediately and clearly pointed out how the interview differed from counseling. Soon after that, he became a lot more comfortable talking to me.

Thirdly, I collected data from a range of individuals (age and gender differences), gathered heterogeneous data (non-verbal and verbal accounts), and used a variety of methods for data analysis (coding, metaphors, analysis and interpretation of sand trays using 2 distinct methods). This hopefully helped "reduce the risk of chance associations and of systematic biases due to a specific method," a strategy known as "triangulation".

Finally, the data were collected and archived in a detailed and complete account for further analysis: Sand trays were photographed and interviews were audiotaped and then transcribed verbatim. Interviews were kept in the language spoken by the participants. Only the quotes used in the final text were translated. Translations were submitted for review to a third party and back-translated. These procedures helped minimize inaccuracy in the description of the data and also facilitated the process of getting feedback from experts and lay persons as I interpreted the data and formulated hypothesis.

Generalizability Issues:

As with most qualitative research projects, this project studied a small, non-random sample of participants. Therefore, generalizing the interpretations and conclusions as representative of people beyond the participants described in this project (external generalizability) was done with much caution. Even so, I anticipated that the conclusions might in fact apply to persons with similar life history even if their voices were not included in this project. That is the argument of those who believe that a well-designed and carried-out qualitative research may have "face generalizability", or the lack of "*obvious* reasons [italics added] *not* to believe that the results apply more generally"(Maxwell, 1996, p. 97). In either case, I did expect that at a minimum, I would be able to determine internal generalizability, which refers to "the generalizability of a conclusion within the setting or group studied" (Maxwell, 1996, p. 97). I believed this was attained, especially because I was able to weigh all participants and their perspectives with equal carefulness.

CHAPTER 4

Stories of the Children Left Behind

In this chapter I will present the 7 participants that were interviewed for this project. Although this study followed a topical design, I found it necessary to describe the participants before introducing the data for three reasons. First, it would provide a contextual background for the presentation and discussion of the findings, the analyses of results, and the final conclusions (addressed in chapters 5, 6, and 7, respectively). Second, it would help the reader identify the person behind each statement. Finally, it would make the reading on findings and data analysis easier to follow.

The reader will notice that the amount and sequence of information provided about each participant does not follow a parallel or similar structure. I chose to present each participant in slightly different and unique ways because I felt that doing so would better reflect my own experience with each of these individuals. Some of these adolescents struck me because of the drama of their life stories while others became memorable because of the way they presented themselves during the interviews. A couple of them were so guarded and distant that at first I thought I did not know them or their stories very well. After reviewing the first draft, in which I described all participants in a linear and similar manner, I realized that the reader would have difficulty telling the participants apart from each other. Whereas I had the advantage of experiencing the participants in a direct way, the readers did not have such opportunity. I felt that it was my responsibility to tell these children's stories in a way that recreated the experience I had as I interviewed and got to know them. I hoped to achieve this goal by modifying the structure of this chapter and choosing a less formal approach to describe the participants. Therefore I start the description of each of these children with what I felt was their most remarkable feature. In addition, the participants who volunteered more information and more stories received more "space" in chapter 4. In contrast, those who seemed unable to recount their stories in detail were described more concisely in this section. By the end of chapter 6, however, the reader will hopefully have a good understanding of all participants in a balanced and equal fashion.

JORGE

Jorge is a tall, heavily built young adult who looks older than his 19 years of age. Yet, there is something childish and naïve about him. His dark hair is shaved from the middle of the skull down to his neck, and his dark skin showed through the tank top shirt he was wearing for the first interview. Jorge was polite but shy. Despite his tough, inner-city dress code, Jorge was almost child-like in the way he related to the interviewer. He was not particularly articulate; many of his answers were monosyllabic, and his thinking was very concrete and matter-of-fact. Surprisingly however, he took great care and was very creative and resourceful as he built the sand trays. Jorge repeatedly asked for permission to use the miniatures sitting on the shelf as he went about the task of building a world on the sand tray.

Jorge's parents seemed to have a good and solid marriage, which was probably a key contributor to his sense of security and peace of mind. His father left El Salvador when Jorge was 8 years old, and his mother joined her husband a year and a half later. Jorge entered the U.S. illegally by crossing the U.S. border by land. At the time of the interviews Jorge was sixteen and worked part time as a waiter. He had never been in therapy and denied any involvement with the legal system.

Jorge is a middle child in a family of six children. He described his childhood as uneventful. However, he saw many deaths and war-related tragedies as a child. He used to have nightmares and he told me that once he arrived to the U.S. and talked to his parents about the nightmares, they were gone. Like many Central American women, Jorge's mother stayed home to care for the children. As a young adult,

Jorge's father was a famous soccer player and later worked on the land as a farmer. He had serious problems with alcohol until Jorge was about 2 years old, but stopped drinking 16 years ago. The family was quite poor but seemed fairly organized. The children had chores and tasks that they were expected to do, and the parents had a good relationship. Jorge was close to his maternal grandparents, who lived nearby, even before the parents' immigration to the U.S.

Jorge was 8 years old when his father decided to immigrate to the U.S., fleeing from the soldiers in El Salvador, who believed him to be a guerrillero (6). Jorge says that at that time, people did not have the right to a trial and that once the militaries believed you were a guerrillero, then your life and that of your family were in danger. Once his father learned that he had been identified as a rebel, he had to flee to save not only his own life, but also to save the lives of all family members. Jorge talked about a family he knew and how they were all killed by soldiers because of rumors that the father in that family was a guerrillero. There was no trial or proof that this was indeed a fact. Jorge believes that if his parents had not left El Salvador, neither they nor the children would be alive today.

Jorge and his siblings were left in the care of the maternal grandmother. Her husband lived nearby, but she decided to move in with her grandchildren after her daughter (Jorge's mother) came to the U.S. One of the maternal uncles also lived in the house and Jorge considered him as a father. Jorge describes the relationship with his grandparents and uncle as close and nurturing.

He described the relationship with his parents as open and caring. He said that he can talk to his parents about anything and that they play around and joke a lot. Jorge denied having any difficulty adjusting to life in the U.S. or being with his parents again. He believes that because he was older when his parents left the process of reunification became easier. Jorge and his entire family were undocumented (7) at the time of the interviews.

Jorge is in 11th grade at a special school for students with a history of behavior problems, interrupted schooling, unspecified learning difficulties, and poor academic performance. Jorge told me that during his years in elementary school, teachers often hit their students. In addition, classes were often cancelled because teachers quit their job in the middle of the school year and there were no arrangements made for replacement. Jorge missed over 2 years of school because of war and teachers leaving the job. This could help to explain the difficulties Jorge reported as he tried to adapt to the American school system. However, Jorge plans to graduate from high school and to work as a "heating and air conditioning" technician.

Jorge reported he had witnessed many atrocities during the years of war in El Salvador. He was not willing to elaborate on the matter, and I decided it would not be ethical or appropriate to pursue that topic any further. Jorge said he saw many dead bodies and "cosas bien feas" (very ugly things). He reported suffering from frequent nightmares while in El Salvador, but that once he talked to his parents about what he had seen, the nightmares were gone.

SUZANA

When I was 6 years old ... I met her [my mother] for the first time [laughs] and it was so funny because they kept showing me pictures, but I never really actually see her, you know? The picture from a person is different sometimes.... I saw her... I will never forget. She was wearing ... the first, first time she went... she was wearing a black dress and she looked like a ... [laughs] she looked like a turkey.... [laughs]. She was wearing a black dress and an overcoat ... and she had a pin right here [showing the collar bone area], but it looked like... Man, I don't know how to explain it. And then I started crying, I was like ... "'That is my Mom!" My aunt was carrying me. "That is my mom, that is my mom!", and then she looked at me and I started crying, and they were like, "Oh, my God, she recognized her mom!". And I kept telling my grandma - cause by then my aunt gave me to my grandma so that she could carry me- and I was, "That is my mom, that is my mom". And then there were bars, like she was in jail, because of immigration. She had to pass all that and then she would hold my hand, and she would not let me go... she would not let go of my hand.

As Suzana spoke to me, she seemed to describe the memories of her childhood as if they were a running movie in her head. Her manners were exuberant and extroverted, and her speech was very rapid.

Suzana is a tall, large, 17 year-old from Colombia with dark skin, and features more typical of African Americans than of Latinos. She was casually dressed in jeans and a T-shirt and did not seem to put much effort in the way she looked. Suzana is a senior in high school and works part-time as an administrative assistant. She does not plan to go to college after graduating from high school and has vague career plans. She enjoys her current job as a customer services representative and intends to work there full-time after graduation. Suzana felt very proud to have bought her own car.

Suzana was very open and eager to talk in detail about her experiences and thoughts on the separation and reunification to her mother in the U.S. She received therapy for about 2 years through a school-based program that offered counseling to students identified as being at risk for dropping out. Suzana and I met a few years ago, during the time I was coordinating that program. Even though we did not interact much at the time, Suzana seemed happy to see me again and to remember about her own therapist and the counseling experience, which took place about 3 years before she was interviewed for this project. This connection seemed to help establish a comfortable and trusting relationship with me right from the start. In addition, I believe that her experience of being in counseling facilitated her feeling at easy with the interview situation. Suzana was already familiar with the concepts of confidentiality and of talking about herself to a stranger.

Suzana's mother was almost 40 years old when Suzana was born, which by Hispanic norms is unusual. She was never married to Suzana's father, although they lived together on occasion. Suzana has no siblings. Suzana was 1 _ years old when her mother immigrated to the U.S.

Suzana's family seems to come from less poor a background than the other participants. On the maternal side, the family owned land and property in Colombia, and Suzana talked at length of how she missed the weekends and vacations she spent with her grandmother at the family's country home. She depicted that house in her first sand tray and there was such a feeling of fullness and liveliness in the tray that even Suzana noticed it and made sure to point that out.

Suzana was left in the care of her maternal grandmother, who often reassured her that the mother came to the U.S. to seek better employment. However, Suzana felt ambivalent and confused about the mother's motives because she never perceived her family as being poor or having financial problems. Suzana also mentioned that, around the time the mother left, her parents' relationship was very difficult. Suzana seemed to be implying that her mother immigrated to escape a failed romance and family conflict. Suzana also resents her father because he told her mother that he would stay in Colombia to take care of Suzana but left her almost immediately after the mother's departure.

> When I was a year old, like, they were having problems in their job, and like, the company broke down, so she [the mother] had to quit, so you know, they got laid off, they had no choice. So she told my father, "leave with me", and he was like, "No, I've got to stay with the baby", you know… and that was all a lie because after my mom left, he moved out. And he never cared for me, like, he would come and visit me like, once a year, and he lived like 5 minutes, 15 minutes away from me. It was not like he lived in the other side of the country, you know?

Suzana was raised by her maternal grandmother, who she considers to know her the most. Suzana proudly told me how she could lie to anybody and get away with it, with exception of her grandmother.

> I mean, my mom doesn't know how I am… and I've been living with her for 7 years. She doesn't know how I am… Nobody knows me better than my grandma and God! That lady has been there since the day I was born… My mom used to go to work and my grandma would baby-sit me… She knows me better than anybody… I mean, she knows me so well … I can't lie to her! I can lie to anybody, I can lie to anybody…

Although the grandmother spanked Suzana on occasion, she described the relationship as always being very close, trustful, and playful. Suzana lived with her grandmother, aunt, uncle, and their children. The aunt and uncle also served as surrogate parents, and Suzana felt loved and included by all of them. Still, there was a sense of shame and of being different because she was not being raised by her mother and because her parents were not married or together.

Suzana immigrated to the U.S. when she was 10 years old. She defined the first two or three years of living with her mother as a "living hell". She felt harshly criticized by her mother and unfairly yelled at. To this day their relationship is fragile, but Suzana says that she has learned to tolerate her mother. Suzana is very suspicious of her parents and has a difficult time trusting others. Despite having heard repeatedly from her grandmother that the mother came to the U.S. to give Suzana a better future, she hesitates to believe it. Suzana also feels resentful and mistrustful of her father. He contacted her shortly after she became an American citizen. As a citizen, she could "sponsor" his application to immigrate to the U.S., that is, to become the responsible party in that process. Suzana was sure that his motivation in trying to reestablish a relationship with her was less than noble; that he was just using her to become a legal resident of the U.S.

ISABELA

Isabela is an attractive, shy, and well-mannered young woman. She has dark, long hair, average height, and typical features of Central Americans with native ancestry. Isabela has had many losses, challenges, and trauma in her short 19 years. And yet, there is a calm and centered energy about her, and she comes across as thoughtful and mature for her age.

Isabela was 9 years old when her mother immigrated to the U.S., leaving the husband and their three children in El Salvador. She was a nurse at the community clinic of the small village where the family lived, and that made the mother a valuable commodity. She had the medical skills and the access to medication the guerrilleros desperately needed during the war. Isabela remembers how her mother was snatched by the guerrilleros in the middle of the night to care for a wounded man. A few days later, she got an anonymous letter threatening that if she did not join the rebels and travel with them to care for the wounded men, she and her entire family would be killed. Although at the time her mother did not explain why she was fleeing the country, Isabela knew all along the kind of danger her mother was facing.

> ... one time, at night, we were... there was a lot of fighting – well, not as much as what my mom went through, but yes, there was a lot. So, I remember one time, in the middle of the night, my mother ... they [rebels] came and she was in her pajamas, and they took her by force and made her go and take care of the wounded and all ... and my mother did not want to go and they told her that they would kill her if she did not go. And my brothers were asleep but I heard when she, when they told her that. So my mom left and didn't come back until the next morning.... and I didn't tell my mother. I pretended that I had not heard anything but I saw my mother crying and I knew she didn't want us to know about what was happening. And then about two days later, they left her an anonymous letter saying that she had to leave her home and everything, and go with them, and that if she didn't go, they would kill her, or us, or something...So my mother felt very bad. And they didn't sign it, no one signed... So my mother told the problem to her sister who lived here, and her sister helped her to go... to come here.

This life and death situation, the war as a common enemy, and the fact that Isabela was old enough to understand what was happening to her mother seemed to help her conceptualize the mother's immigration as a sacrifice she made for the survival of her entire family. After the mother's departure, Isabela and her two younger siblings went to live in an orphanage. Isabela and her sister were sent to boarding school for girls, and the brother to a school for boys. Their father worked in another town and they had no family available to care for them. On weekends the children went home and spent time with the father. Isabela was very close to her father and saw him as a caring man who was very invested in his family. However, when asked who she felt raised her during the 8 years of separation, Isabela could not identify any particular person.

Isabela described the nuns who ran the orphanage as very strict, but caring. She seemed glad to have had the opportunity to learn a range of skills while at the orphanage, including cooking and sewing. The alternative would have been to wander the streets after school, like other orphans did. Isabela also valued the discipline and structure that the orphanage provided.

When Isabela was 12 years old, she and her two siblings moved back to the family's home. Now Isabela was not only in charge of herself, but was also responsible for her then 11 year-old brother, David, and 10 year-old sister, Patricia. The father continued to work at another town and to come home on weekends. Isabela says that the family planed to reunite, but their plans changed unexpectedly. One day Isabela received the visit of her father's coworkers, who came to take the children to the town where her father worked. Isabela's father had been shot and killed during a robbery at his work. She was fifteen.

> His boss sent two of his workers to pick us up, and they told us that ... I don't know, that it seems that my father was ill and that we had to go see him. And we left, just as we were [dressed]. And when we arrived at the place he worked, we saw a cousin of ours... and she liked my father very much. My father was like a father to her. So, when I saw that she was crying, I knew that there was something wrong. Then she said that my father no longer existed, and my sister started to cry, and she continued to talk, but I don't know ... I was in shock; a nervous shock. She was talking but I couldn't hear what she was saying. And I couldn't cry. I wanted to cry, but I couldn't. And I didn't want to see, and it all seemed to be a joke, but then when I saw him.... I mean, it was as if I couldn't believe it. And then my brother, I mean, I didn't feel bad for myself, but more for my brother, you know? Because we, me and my sister, the two of us were, we supported each other, and all ... But he, he was a boy and he had nobody to help him.

Isabela seemed very distressed over the fact that she could not cry, which was mentioned at other times during our meetings. She also felt overwhelmed in her new role of sole caretaker of her younger siblings. With her mother in the U.S. and her father deceased, the world became a much more dangerous place.

Isabela and her sibling went to a city nearby to attend the father's funeral and asked one of their aunts to watch the house for a few days. Upon their return they found that all their belonging stolen. This seemed to be very traumatic for Isabela, and she became quite emotional as she described the event. Maybe she saw it as proof that now, without the protection of her father or her mother, she and her siblings were alone and at the mercy of fate as they tried to survive in an unsafe, unkind world. Another traumatic event described by Isabela was the bombing of her classroom during the time she was living at the orphanage. She suffered some injuries that required medical attention. She was hospitalized for a couple of days and was in bed rest for sometime as she returned to the orphanage. Although being hurt was traumatic for her, coming in contact with children who had been seriously injured seemed to represent a more traumatic experience for her. Contrary to my expectations, Isabela did not mention a desire to be with her mother as she recovered from her injuries. It has been my clinical observation that children will long for their mother or main caretaker's protection when feeling sick or vulnerable. Instead, Isabela talked about how her schoolmates took care of her and brought her food while she was at the school infirmary.

After her father's death, Isabela and her siblings moved in with an aunt and her family. Although Isabela did not get into much detail about that period during our interview, I had the feeling that living with that family was not pleasant. Two years after her husband's death, Isabela's mother was able to bring the children to the U.S. Isabela was 17 and, by then, she had been separated from her mother for 8 years.

Isabela is now 19 years old, married, and mother of a 10 month-old girl. She became pregnant soon after the marriage. Isabela lives with her husband of two years and their young daughter. The husband is also from El Salvador and works long hours in construction. Isabela lives next to her mother and feels very close to her, almost to an unhealthy extent. For example, when Isabela was first married, she and her husband moved to a town about 20 miles from her mother's home. Isabela mentioned a few times during the interview how difficult it was for her not to be able to see her mother every day. She felt very lonely and spent hours talking on the phone with her mom. She finally convinced her husband to move to the same apartment complex as her mother. She now spends most of her time with her mother.

Isabela described the relationship with her mother as always being very close and trusting. She saw the mother as her best friend before the mother's immigration. Although Isabela did not get into great detail about the first months after the reunification, there seemed to be a period when she felt more distant and less trusting of the mother. She mentioned how it is now her younger sister's turn to be rebellious and difficult, implying that there was a time when Isabela 's behavior was somewhat challenging. However, that seemed short-lived, and Isabela told me she felt very close to her mother and adapted well to her own role as a wife and mother.

While in El Salvador, Isabela's parents held semi-skilled jobs and seemed to place priority in the children's education. Isabela is enrolled in 11th grade at a high school with special arrangements for teenage mothers, but she does not receive special education services. Isabela plans to become a nurse, like her mother. Isabela said that although she enjoyed learning and being in school while living in El Salvador, she has not done well in American schools, and had much difficulty learning English. Her younger brother and sister, on the other hand, have not adjusted as well as she has. Isabela's brother, David, and her younger sister, Patricia, have had many runs with the law and are probably involved in gangs. David is now living out-of-state, in what seems to be the mother's effort to keep him away from gangs and criminal activity. Patricia has been held in the local juvenile detention center more than once.

Isabela seemed to put much effort in the way she dressed for the interviews, and her clothes were somewhat fancy for the occasion. I interpreted such care as a sign that she saw the interviews as important and a special event. My impression was confirmed by how thoughtful and serious she was in answering my questions, and how much effort she made to relay a complete and accurate picture of her life history. She also must have talked about the project to her friends, because in our second meeting Isabela offered me the name of two other teenagers with a history of separation, and who wanted to be interviewed for this project. By that time, however, I had already identified all the participants and did not contact her friends.

Although Isabela was shy at first, she was surprisingly assertive and forthcoming at times. She was the one to request to participate in this project, for example. At first I was given the name of her younger sister as a possible interviewee. Patricia had been identified through a school-based counseling program where she received counseling services. When I called the mother's home, asking for Patricia, Isabela answered the phone and volunteered that Patricia had spoken to her about the project and that she also wanted to be interviewed. As it turned out, Patricia was detained shortly after the phone call, and was never interviewed for this project.

Isabela often surprised me with her keen insight and intuitive understanding about human nature. When asked whether she would like to have other children, she laughed as she noted how much work it takes to raise a child. Then, she added that she would wait until her daughter was older because, in her own experience, having to share the mother's attention with her younger siblings was difficult. In a pensive voice she added that, in her view, children need special care and attention until about the age of 5. When asked where she got that idea from, she told me, "through experience and observation."

Isabela was emotionally open and took great risk in sharing information and expressing her emotions during the interviews. She seemed to feel trusting and comfortable with me. I believe that one of the things that helped make her feel comfortable was the opportunity to chitchat during the car ride from her house to the office where the interview took place. This in fact, was a perfect icebreaker for all the participants to whom I provided transportation.

RITA

Rita is an attractive adolescent with long, dark hair, light skin, and average build. Of all participants, she was the one experiencing the most difficulty and distress in the relationship with her mother. Even though Suzana and Alex (described later in this chapter) had much difficulty during the first couple of years following reunification with their parents, they seemed to have integrated and worked through some of their frustrations over the years, and were now better able to relate to their parents. They were older, and their age may also have played an important role in their ability to internalize and negotiate their emotions. Rita on the other hand, was trying to cope and adjust to all the relatively recent life changes at the time she was interviewed for this project.

At times, as Rita told me her life story, she presented with a somewhat childish speech, and she was reticent and somewhat disorganized as she spoke about emotional issues. However, when describing less emotionally charged material, her thinking was clear and concise. Rita seemed to have so much unexpressed grief and sadness around the experience of separation and reunification to her mother that I often felt the need to change to the role of a therapist during the interviews. Although for the most part I avoided to take on that role, I also felt that in a couple of occasions she was so distressed that it would only be ethical and appropriate to try to contain her affect, which I did.

I first met Rita about 2 years before starting this project, when her mother was seeking counseling for Rita at the mental health center I worked at the time. After an initial evaluation, I referred Rita and her mother to one of the therapists for family counseling. They attended family sessions for about two months and then dropped out of treatment. Rita was 16 when she was interviewed for this project.

Rita is the older of two girls, born to a boyfriend the mother had back in El Salvador. Her parents never married, but lived together at times, and they seemed to have a difficult, possibly abusive relationship. Rita's father was not much involved in raising the children and was not accepted by the mother's family. Rita lived with her mother, her sister, and her maternal grandmother for most of her childhood, including the time prior to the mother's immigration. Rita felt ashamed of her mother's single status and wished that her parents were married and together. She said that she constantly compared herself to her friends, who she felt had a happier and more stable life because their parents were married.

> You see, in Latin America … if you have a stepfather, a stepmother, people think you as different because your parents are not together… So, I did not have my father nor my mother, but instead I lived with my uncles. And everybody talked about their mothers, and with my friends, I did not know what to talk about it because I was not living with my mother. So, then, it was hard for me… Yeah…

Rita was 7 years old when her mother came to the U.S. She believes that her mother decided to immigrate following a family fight around inheritance and division of money between Rita's mother and her siblings. The family owned a restaurant and one of Rita's uncles advised the grandmother to keep his sister (Rita's mother) from inheriting any part of it. Rita said that the family conflict and rejection led her mother to immigrate. However, Rita could not understand the mother's decision to leave because unlike other parents that leave their children behind, her family did not experience any financial difficulties or problems related to the civil war;. "No, I mean ... I did not think about it because I know that people come here because of poverty, or because of the wars in El Salvador ... But my mother had everything!"

In addition to the absence of a strong reason to immigrate, Rita's mother did not tell her that she was leaving to the U.S., and she did not say goodbye. Then, for years the family made up stories every time that Rita asked about her mother, often reassuring her that the mother was in a city nearby and that she would soon return. Rita talked of how she waited, and waited, until she stopped believing in adults. The secrecy and unfortunate mishandling of the situation seemed to contribute to Rita's distress over the separation and the ending result was her chronic anxiety and distrust in adults. Similar circumstances and ending results were also observed in other children I interviewed for this project. In their effort to protect the children from their loss, grandparents and other caretakers often made matters worse as they confused these children with their misinformation and half-lies.

Rita described being very clingy to her mother before the mother's immigration, despite being harshly punished by her at times. She says that although the separation from the mother was very hard on her, her life in fact became easier after the mother's departure because, unlike her mother, the grandmother and uncles did not hit or yell at her. After the mother's departure, Rita and her sister went to live with her grandmother, who cared for them until Rita was 12, when the grandmother died. Rita says that her grandmother treated her well, but she did not seemed to feel particularly close to her.

After the grandmother's death, Rita and her sister went to live with an uncle, his wife, and their children. Rita described the next two years as the best time in her life. She felt loved and protected by the couple, and was pleased to be part of a family that was a better match to her idealization of a family, where mother and father are married and raising their children together. Rita confided in her aunt and felt very close to her.

At age 14, Rita immigrated to the U.S., brought by her mother. Upon her arrival, she was surprised to learn that the mother had re-married a few years earlier. Again, Rita was not informed about important events in her mother's life. In addition, the relationship between Rita's mother and her new husband was abusive up until the girls joined them, and Rita often took the role of the mother's confidant, which increased her feelings of anxiety and distress.

Rita and her mother were experiencing much difficulty as they tried to adjust to each other. The mother often criticized the uncle and aunt who took care of Rita for two years before her immigration, and prohibited Rita from talking to or about them. Rita's mother seemed to feel threatened whenever Rita mentioned her aunt and uncle. Being forbidden to express her grief over the loss of that relationship made the transition to living in the U.S. even harder for Rita, and at the time of this interview, she presented as anxious and depressed.

Rita cried several times during the interviews, as she talked about the aunt and uncle she lived with from ages 12 to 14, and to whom she felt very attached. She also cried when she spoke of her difficulty relating to her mother. Rita described her mother as very impulsive and emotionally volatile, and she believed that the mother's history of abuse had left her bitter and angry.

> I don't know, because when my mother came to this country, she suffered a little with her husband. He, it seems that, hum... he treated her badly... and now, now that I came, my mother is a bitter woman [very expressive, resigned tone]... and she is a woman ... <u>completely</u> ... [emphatic] she is not the same. She is a, a ... she is not bitter all the time, but most of the time, she is always bitter. Sometimes, she gets angry for little things ... because of one little thing, and she screams. These are the times that she cannot control herself.

LUIS

Luis is a tall, slender teenager with dark hair and dark skin. He was neatly dressed and his manners were polite but reserved. At the time of these interviews, Luis was 15. He was born in El Salvador, and his parents separated shortly after his birth. Luis believes that the separation was caused by his father's alcoholism. He says that he doesn't remember his father being drunk because he was always "normal" when he came to visit the children on the weekends. As a child, Luis never had much contact with his father. Luis is the youngest of 6 children and was attending 9th grade at a local high school when these interviews took place. He was enrolled in English as a Second Language (ESL) classes, and planned to graduate from high school and work with computers.

Luis did not seem ready or open to explore his feelings around the experience of separation from and reunification with his mother. His answers were brief and matter-of-fact, and even when asked to tell me a particular story or to elaborate on some information, he seemed unable to explore beyond basic facts. Much like Jorge, however, Luis was creative and resourceful as he worked with the miniatures and sand tray. Whereas the two teenagers had some difficulty expressing verbally, when it came to the sand tray task, they were motivated, involved, and able to bring together elaborate concepts and images.

Luis was 6 years old when his mother decided to immigrate to the U.S. She had difficulty feeding the six children on the low wages she earned in El Salvador. The mother's plan, according to Luis, was to either send for the children or to return within 3 years, but that never happened. It wasn't until 6 years later that Luis was able to join the mother in the U.S. In fact, two of Luis's younger siblings were still in El Salvador at the time of this interview, and Luis lived in an apartment complex with his mother and two older siblings.

Between the ages of 6 and 12, Luis and his siblings were left in the care of the maternal grandmother. Prior to the mother's immigration, Luis lived with his grandmother, mother, and siblings. Luis felt very close to his grandmother, and he still considers her to be the person who raised him. It seems that his childhood was stable and he felt loved and cared for by his grandmother. Luis described the current relationship with his mother as respectful and that he confides in her for almost everything. Luis was very fond of the fact that, when he arrived in the U.S., he and his mother spent almost the whole night chatting and comparing notes about how different their journey to the U.S. turned out to be. Both of them were brought to the U.S. by *coyotes*: individuals who get paid to get immigrants across the border illegally. However, whereas the mother's trip seemed full of danger and deprivation, Luis felt as if he was on a tour, stopping at Macdonald's and sleeping at motels with clean sheets and hot showers. Luis's father had recently arrived in the U.S., but he did not live with the family. Luis told me that he was beginning to know his father, and that he enjoyed talking to him about things he felt would be inappropriate to discuss with his mother. He denied any problems or feelings of abandonment as result of the mother's immigration.

Luis said that he still misses his grandmother, but that when he arrived, after two weeks of being with his mother he already felt very comfortable. The only exception to his quick and easy adaptation to the U.S. and to his mother seemed to be adapting to the school system and a new language. For example, Luis talked about how he missed the school bus a couple of times because he did not know which bus to enter when school was out. Despite much prompting, Luis did not bring out any examples or events that might illustrate further his reactions to moving to the U.S.

CARLA

Carla was highly motivated to participate in this project, in great part because she had plans to work with children in a mental health or counseling-related field. She hoped that talking with me would be helpful as she tried to learn more about the mental health profession.

Carla is an attractive 19 year-old, who presented at first as mature and articulate. However, her narrative tended to be unfocused and over-inclusive, and she often digressed into unrelated facts. Although Carla tried to come across as self-assured and analytical, her thinking was often nebulous. Her speech was very rapid and she mumbled. Carla had never been in therapy, and she was anxious and overly dramatic as she told me her story. Carla had difficulty accepting a casual compliment or apology - possibly the result of cultural norms that emphasize humbleness and modesty; but she was also solicitous and seemed eager to please. Dressed in jeans and shirt, her appearance was neat but unremarkable. Carla is tall and slender, has dark, long hair, and light skin. At the time of the interview she was a senior, and felt ashamed for being in high school at her age.

Carla is the oldest of three children, and her parents were very young when her mother became pregnant. Carla believes that the pregnancy forced the parents to quit school and start working. Her parents never married, but they lived together from the time Carla was born until when she was about 2 years old. Her brother was a baby when the parents separated. Carla's mother came to the U.S. when Carla was 6 years old, leaving her and her brother in El Salvador, in the care of the grandmother and uncles. Carla's father was never well accepted into the mother's family, but when Carla was about 15, the father started visiting the children more often, and they became close. A year later Carla joined her mother in Virginia. She is now 19, and has been in the U.S. for the past 3 years. Carla also has a 6 year-old half brother. He is autistic.

Congruent with cultural norms, family loyalty is a fundamental value in Carla's family. She told me that her grandparents had some land and wealth, but that everything was lost or stolen during the years of civil war in El Salvador, and that the family was left in extreme poverty. There were times when they did not have enough to eat. Being the oldest child, Carla's mother was expected to help raise the younger siblings as well as her two children. So, her mother immigrated first to the U.S., helped pay for the education of her younger siblings, and then slowly brought each of them to the U.S.. Carla was very critical of one of her uncles, who after getting through school with her mother's help, failed to do his part and help other family members get ahead. Instead, he got married and distanced himself from his family of origin.

Carla's mother decided to immigrate after struggling to keep her two children and several younger brothers and sisters from starving. She came to the U.S. with another woman, a friend of hers. She lived with a family and cared for their children for many years. Much like Rita, Carla was told that the mother was in a nearby town working, and it was not until a couple of years later that she was told that her mother was in the U.S.

During the 10 years they were separated from their mother, Carla and her brother were cared for by her grandmother. Although Carla denied a history of abuse or neglect, it seems that she never felt connected to any of her caretakers or to her mother before, during, and after the period of separation. Carla described the relationship with her mother as being always respectful, but distant.

Carla is attending 12th grade and takes school very seriously. While living in El Salvador, Carla's dream was to attend a school that had a reputation for its high academic standards. During our interview, Carla spoke at great length about how hard she worked to be accepted at that school, and how happy and accomplished she felt when she not only got accepted, but actually received a scholarship. After attending the school of her dreams for a few weeks, Carla's immigration papers finally came through, and she felt she had no choice but come to the U.S. She felt it would have been a betrayal of her mother's sacrifice to decline the opportunity to immigrate. Carla described the period of adaptation to the American school system and to life and in the U.S. as the most stressful experience of her life. She felt incompetent because of her lack of English skills. At the same time, however, she felt being held back academically because the material she was being introduced to at American school was a repetition of what she had learned years before in El Salvador. At times, Carla feared that she would not be able to learn the language or graduate from high school. There seemed to be an unspoken anxiety of repeating her parents' fate, as they had failed to graduate from high school. To make things worse, the relationship between Carla and her mother was very tense and unfulfilling, particularly in the first 2 or 3 years after the reunification.

Although Carla seemed bright and motivated, her emotional distress seemed to play an important role in keeping her level of anxiety very high and her thoughts scattered and disorganized. However, Carla seemed able to compartmentalize her distress and reported to be doing well in school and to have learned English very quickly. After 3 years of being in the U.S., she is beginning to see the positive aspects of a life with more opportunities, especially for women who, like her, have ambitious career goals.

ALEX

Alex is a personable, polite, and charming 18 year-old Guatemalan with dark hair, light skin, and an open, friendly smile. He was very energetic and "upbeat" at both meetings, and seemed to put much effort to come across as a carefree, sociable young adult. Alex was very polite and solicitous, but also anxious, particularly during the first interview. His twin-sister had previously been in counseling with me, and Alex seemed concerned about being perceived as psychologically disturbed or "abnormal" in any way. For example, when asked to build a world by placing miniatures in a sand tray, he jokingly asked whether the interview was in fact a counseling session. At another point, Alex volunteered that he never understood why his sister Martha had been referred for treatment. During our second meeting, however, Alex was more at ease with the interview process and more willing to talk about his feelings and thoughts instead of trying to sell me a trouble-free picture of his life. At the end of the meetings, he told me that this was the first time he talked to anyone about his experience of separation and reunification with his parents, and that he found the process to be very helpful.

Alex's family was quite poor in Guatemala, but through years of hard work the family attained some financial stability in the U.S. Alex was three months old when his father left to the U.S., seeking better employment and higher wages. For the next 2 years Alex lived in Guatemala with his mother, older sister, and twin sister, Martha. Then, his mother immigrated to the U.S. to join her husband, leaving the children with the paternal grandmother and 3 cousins whose parents had also left to the U.S.. Five years ago, Alex and his three sisters immigrated to the U.S.. Alex was thirteen and he had been separated from his mother for 11 years. He had never lived with his father.

Alex said that he felt loved and nurtured by his grandmother and that to this day he feels very attached to her. He was also close to one of his uncles, who he looked up to as a father. Alex, his two siblings, and their three cousins were very close, but much like other twins, Alex and Martha seem to enjoy a particularly close relationship. Alex talked about his childhood as a stable and happy time in his life. When he was about 6 years old, his grandmother's house caught on fire. Nobody was injured, but seeing the grandmother's arms and legs burnt was a traumatic experience for Alex and his sisters. His grandmother was hospitalized for about 3 months. Afterwards they moved to a larger home thanks to the money Alex's parents sent to the family.

Alex's father had a history of alcoholism and did not work for long periods of time. In fact, due to his alcoholism, his father lost a job that would have provided the opportunity for the whole family to get residency status. Therefore, Alex reasoned, the father's alcoholism was to blame for the delay in the children's immigration to the U.S. Alex tried to make this event humorous and light, referring to those days as the father's "vacation years". However, he did seem to have mixed feelings about coming to the U.S. at a later age, which he felt made learning a new language all the more difficult. Although Alex still idealizes his father, he felt much shame and anger when he learned, about 2 years ago, that his father had another son. That boy is about Alex's age.

Alex described the first three years following his arrival in the U.S. as very difficult. He and his sisters were constantly fighting with the parents, who were seen as strict and untrusting of them. Communication was poor, and Alex missed his cousins and grandmother terribly. He and his sisters took turns acting out and being the focus of attention in their fights with the parents.

Alex described the current relationship with his mother as respectful, formal, and emotionally distant, but he used words such as "joking" and "playing around" to characterize his relationship with his grandmother and his father. Alex thought his mother was "funny" in the way she believed that playfulness feeling comfortable around a parent was an invitation for disrespect and an unacceptable break down in the family hierarchy.

At the time of the interview Alex was attending 11th grade, and although he did not receive special education services, he was still enrolled in ESL classes. He planned to graduate from high school and start his own construction company with a cousin of his. He would also like to eventually graduate from a construction management program offered by a local university.

COMMON THREADS

In summary, these children's stories had several elements in common, and as expected, patterns began to emerge. All of the participants were young children when the mother or the parents left, and most did not reunite with their parent or parents until they entered adolescence. Most participants witnessed war-related events or were, at the very least, affected by the civil wars in Central America. Most of the children interviewed were left in the care of grandparents, uncles, and aunts. It was not uncommon that the surrogate caretakers of the children interviewed were also in charge of other children (usually the participants' cousins), whose parents had also immigrated to the U.S. Most of the children, and especially those born to single mothers, had been living with their grandparents even before the parents' immigration. Finally, many of these families seemed unprepared to explain to these children what was happening as the parents immigrated.

CHAPTER 5
The Times of Separation

A mother's job is to be there to be left.
Anna Freud

In this chapter I will focus on the participant's answers to the topics covered during the first of the two interviews, in which I asked them to elaborate on their memory about the years they were separated from their parent or parents. I will present and discuss relevant segments of the interviews identified through the two methods of data analysis used in this project: coding and sand tray analysis. I will address the four main research questions that helped guide this project. Briefly stated, they were: (1) How did children understand and integrate the experience of being left behind as the parent or parents immigrate to the U.S.? (2) What was the impact of that event and its interpretation in their representational model of self? (3) What was the impact of that event and its interpretation in their representational model of others?, and finally, (4) What was the impact of the separation in the participants' emotional development?

In addressing these questions and presenting the findings, I chose not to subdivide the participants in subgroups. I also chose not to organize the presentation of findings around the group of children who adapted well versus those who adapted poorly to the separation from their parents. Instead, I chose to present the participants either individually or as one group.

Three main reasons contributed to my decision to present the participants individually at times, and as a whole group at other times. First, the sample size in this study was too small to effectively subdivide the participants into subgroups and then to confidently reach conclusions based on the variables observed in those subgroups. It seems that such attempt would become an open invitation to the criticism of those who (understandably) might question the validity of my conclusions. Secondly, the set of variables seemed too great and too complex to effectively and clearly separate the participants into subgroups: For example, there were individual personality traits and characteristics to consider, specific family dynamics and circumstances, environmental and historical factors, specific life events that influenced in different degrees how the participants presented themselves, and specific strategies participants used to deal with the life events imposed upon them. Finally, there has been virtually no previous research on this topic and with this particular population that could serve as guide for this project.

Coding was the main method of analysis used to support the findings, discussion, and conclusions. Certain segments of the interviews were identified and coded because they formed important patterns of response across participants, leading to the creation of coding categories. Narrative and sand tray analyzes were used as complimentary methods of analysis. In some instances, they validated and brought further evidence to support the conclusions reached through the analysis of the coding categories. In other cases, they helped to detect internal contradictions in the participants' report, leading to further questions and conclusions. These two additional methods of analysis were helpful in adding another dimension to my understanding of these children's perspective and their efforts to internalize and come to terms with the choices their parents made.

In chapters 5 and 6, I will weave the three types of analyzes used in this project. By the end of chapter 5, the reader will hopefully have a better understanding of how the internal and external events these children experienced during the period of separation shaped their perceptions about their parents, helped create their internal working models self and others, and contributed to their emotional development.

Table 3. Coding Categories Used for Analysis

FREE NODES (8)	TREE NODES (9)		
	DAMAGED GOODS	HEROES	LOVE
Abandonment	Culture as damaged	Culture as hero	Food
Career			Money
Competency	Parents as damaged	Parents as heroes	Playing
Divided Loyalties			Presents
Trauma	Self as damaged	Self as hero	Punishment
War			Talking
Sibling bonding	Life as damaged	Life as hero	Going out
Shame			Respect
School			Spoiled
Sacrifice			
Role Reversal			
Losses			
Guilt			

ABANDONMENT OR SACRIFICE?

The main question I hoped to address in this project was how adolescent Latinos separated from their parents in childhood gave meaning to that experience. Did they see it as sacrifice or abandonment? What caused them to internalize the parent's behavior as sacrifice for the children or outright abandonment?

I had some general ideas about preliminary coding categories that might emerge from the data. However, congruent with the interpretative method of data analysis, I also allowed for many of the coding categories to evolve from the data itself. I identified and coded segments that directly referred to the research questions, such as *sacrifice* and *abandonment*, but I also found that specific themes and patterns repeated themselves across participants. Some of them were directly related to the main topic of this project and some were not, but were worth of being coded and/or analyzed. Consequently, some coding categories generated from the data do not fit neatly any research question. There is some overlap in the coding categories, and approximations were sometimes necessary for pulling the data analysis together. The coding categories most useful to address the   first research question are presented in Table 4.

Table 4. Coding Categories: Abandonment or Sacrifice?

FREE NODES	TREE NODES		
	DAMAGED GOODS	HEROES	LOVE
Abandonment	Self as damaged	Self as hero	Food
Sacrifice			Money
Divided Loyalties	Parents as damaged	Parents as heroes	Playing
Role Reversal			Presents
Losses	Life as damaged	Life as hero	Punishment
Guilt			Talking
Shame			Going out
			Respect
			Spoiled

Two elements seemed to be the most decisive in guiding the children's interpretation of the parents' reasons to immigrate: life events and external circumstances (context), and the parents' dependability to contact and provide for the children while separated.

CONTEXTUAL FACTORS: IN SEARCH OF A COMMON ENEMY AND A BETTER LIFE

Participants who believed that parents immigrated to free the family from poverty, to escape from war, or a combination of the two seemed more likely to interpret the parent's decision as a sacrifice they made to offer their children and family a better life and a better future. Participants who perceived the family as united and fighting against an external, common enemy, found it easier to justify and accept the parent's decision to immigrate. Furthermore, if caretakers and the immediate community, such as school, friends, and neighbors, reinforced the explanations and interpretation of the parent's motives, then these children were less likely to feel rejected or abandoned by the parents.

Poverty and War

Among the participants of this project, extreme poverty and hardship were reported as the main and most common reason for the parent or parents to immigrate. Almost all parents told these children that they were coming to the U.S. to seek a better future for the children. If the children were repeatedly told that the family was very poor before the parent's immigration, then it was easier for them to internalize the belief that the parent came to the U.S. to rescue the family from hunger and suffering. In some cases, the children were old enough to be aware and remember how poor the family actually was before the parents' immigration. That seemed to make it even easier for them to interpret the event as a sacrifice the parents made for their sake. Jorge, Carla, and Luis were old enough to remember how sparse resources were before the mother's departure. Alex was only 2 years old at the time his father and mother left. He did not remember being poor, but he does remember his grandmother constantly reinforcing the idea that the parents were working hard in the U.S. to give him and his sisters a better life. When asked why he thought his parents came to the U.S., Alex simply said, "to give us a better life".

Jorge remembers in very precise and concrete terms the improvements in the family's living conditions soon after his father immigrated. To him, such improvements were clear evidence that his father was in the U.S. to attend to the family's needs.

At the time my dad first got here, we lived in an adobe house, adobe, with aluminum sheets. But then after some time working here and saving, he contracted a brick house for us. And then it all changed. We were doing well.

In Carla's case, poverty was brought by the civil war.

> In reality, we did not have... at the village where we lived, my family, we were left with almost nothing because of the war. We had absolutely nothing. The land my grandmother, my grandparents had, they took. The house we had in the countryside, all of it. They took it all at once, and we were left with nothing. I believe it all started to get worse in 1980. And then, my grandfather, he died in 1982, from disappointment, I believe, and basically, we had nothing, absolutely nothing.

Congruent with cultural norms and expectations, family members were counted upon to pull together in times of hardship. Older brothers and sisters had to take on the responsibility to put the younger siblings through school. Carla's mother immigrated to help not only her own children, but also her brothers and sisters.

> She [my mother] is one of 10 siblings . . . My uncles, my mother's brothers, came to an agreement; "Some of you will graduate, because you are young, and the older ones will go to another city to work and provide for us". Because it was very difficult. And the younger ones would continue studying. Because even though we were poor, we had to study. And that is when my mother said, "I will go first to the U.S.." So she came and started to send us [money]. And her first paycheck went to us, to my brother and I. And then, an older uncle came to the U.S. So, starting in '87, I think that if it wasn't for my mother, or for an uncle, we would be with nothing. But since then, they would send us money to buy this, pay for that; build that . . . And as they graduated, they started working.

Yet, at some level Carla seemed ambivalent about the mother's decision. After trying to explain to me (and therefore, to herself), why her mother immigrated to the U.S., Carla stated without much assurance, "Her reason? I don't know ... maybe so that she could make a better life for her and for her children; maybe."

Fleeing war:
During the 1970's and 1980's, life in several Central American countries was disturbed by civil war, and some parents felt they had to leave to save their lives and/or the lives of their family. Whereas some were identified as being *guerrilleros* (rebels), others were seen as having skills the guerrileros desperately needed. As mentioned in the previous chapter, Isabela's mother was taken out of the house in the middle of the night to care for wounded rebels. In addition, she was coerced by the guerrileros to steal supplies from the clinic where she worked.

> She [my mother] worked at the community health clinic there. The rebels did not have medicines or anything, and they forced my mother to take the medicine from the clinic, because my mother had the keys and everything. And my mom was afraid, and that is why she did it, took it, and all. And then, where we lived, in that community, people were accusing my mother of stealing the medicine, and the other nurse, my mother's coworker, they took both of them. So my mother was desperate. Maybe I was only 9; maybe I couldn't understand it very well, but I knew what was going on. So, this friend of my mother, she had to go... she had to come also.

Even in the language she uses, Isabela makes it clear to the listener that the mother and her friend had no choice but flee the country. Isabela refers to the mother's departure with the expression "she *had* to come", describes the mother as being *desperate,* and being *forced* to steal medical supplies at work. It is clear that Isabela saw her mother as a victim of external forces, with no choice but to flee for her life.

Unlike Isabela, Jorge did not learn the true reasons behind his parents' immigration until five years later, when his grandparents told him and his brothers what really happened. The grandparents feared that if the children knew the truth at a younger age, they might talk to outsiders and put the whole family in danger of persecution or retaliation. Although Jorge also uses strong expressions, such as that the father had to come to the U.S., his narrative alternates between facts and explanations. It seems that Jorge is trying to create an internal guide for himself and for the listener on how to interpret the events. It could also be that Jorge is unconsciously trying to protect himself and his parents against the unpleasant feelings of abandonment, rejection, and resentment toward his parents by convincing himself that his grandparents were indeed telling him the truth.

> They [the grandparents] told us when I was already 14. And they did not trust us because when one is young, one says things ... things one shouldn't say. So, when they felt pressured, they told us the truth ... so that we wouldn't lose the love for our parents. So, when they told us, the reason was that they, the soldiers, thought that my father was one of them [guerrileros], and they were looking for my father to kill him. So, he had to leave the country [pause]. He had to leave the country and my mom, out of fear, she wasn't staying there either.

Fleeing poverty:

For Luis, the family's poverty and the mother having to raise six children on her own were enough reasons to make her leave. Luis talked about how the salary his mother was paid in El Salvador was just not enough to feed the entire family. His story, however, seems to parrot the explanations given by his grandmother. Somehow, it sounds as if it is coming from an adult rather than being generated by his young mind.

> Yes, we did not have a good house, as they say, we did not have a good home. And she... and she worked and they did not pay her well. And as we were 6 children, and she alone, it was a great effort to raise the children, and that is why she said she was going to come to this country. She wanted us to have a better life, not to go through the same things, poor. Yes, a better future for us. To give us an education and all...

When parents have everything:

However, for those who did not experience poverty and war, the parent's immigration kept them perplexed. In the cases of Rita and Suzana, neither financial needs nor war were an issue. This seemed to greatly contribute to their feeling rejected when their mothers decided to leave. In her confusion, Rita's strategy was to refuse to think about it altogether. "I did not think about it [the reason for my mother to immigrate] because all the people that come here is because of poverty or because of the wars in El Salvador... And my mother had everything!"

Suzana tried to make sense of the bits and pieces her grandmother told her and of how she felt about the mother's departure. Yet, she could not really come to terms with the fact that her mother decided to leave her and come to the U.S. In addition, Suzana experienced her mother as very critical and their relationship became very conflictual once Suzana moved to the U.S. That seemed to increase the feelings of rejection and abandonment that she struggled to put aside as a child.

> ...my grandma showed me pictures, saying "this is your Mom, you got love her, she loves you really much, she left because...", you know, like... when I was a year old, they were having problems in their job, and the company broke down, so she had to quit. They got laid off, they had no choice. I used to resent her, because I used to think maybe she didn't love, you know... that it was just an excuse, that she left me, you know? Because, I mean, we as kids don't see everything right. I used to think, probably she left me and she never cared for me....

Suzana also talked about how believing that her mother was living a life of luxury in the U.S., a childhood perception that later proved misleading, made it more difficult for her to think of her mother as making a sacrifice. Furthermore, once Suzana realized that such perception was false, she then felt guilty for thinking of the mother as being rich when in fact she was living quite uncomfortably, supposedly so that Suzana could be comfortable. Instead of seeing the misunderstanding as simply poor communication, Suzana internalized the blame and thought of herself as ungrateful and "spoiled". That, in turn, added to her feelings of anger and resentment towards the mother.

> Because my aunt and my mom worked so hard to build a house ... Because we had like, a two-story house, it has 4 bathrooms and everything, you know? ... our house ... So

they used to be, "You, rich little spoiled girl who had
everything". They used to think that my mom was wealthy and
rich. Even I used to think that! I used to think, "Uau, my mom
is rich!" Why? Because of all the money she was spending
.... But I never knew the truth, that she lived in a little
apartment, you know? Uncomfortable ... because over there
[in Colombia] see ... because this is what parents don't tell
you; they never show you the real thing, like, how they suffer
... or anything. So, how can you know? I would think that ...
I used to think that she was here with another husband, you
know? I used to think that she never loved me; that she left
me there.

As Suzana spoke those last words, she started to cry. She seemed
torn between feelings of rejection and abandonment, and guilt over
being perceived as selfish and ungrateful. Although her interpretation
of the events seem extreme, leading to unresolved grief and possibly
depression, most of the participants seemed to fall somewhere along
this continuum. Even for children who showed little internal conflict
over the reasons why the parent had to immigrate, there was always a
lingering doubt, and the feeling that just maybe they did not deserve
their parent's affection.

It seems that caretakers and children were constantly grasping for
details that gave proof of the mother's departure as a sacrifice. One
metaphor used by a couple of the participants was related to enduring
the cold weather and snow. Isabela mentioned snow in the context of
sacrifice;

He [my father] used to tell us that we should not think badly of
my mother because he knew that maybe she was having a hard
time here [in the U.S.]. He would make us watch the news,
when there was a snow storm here and all, and he would tell
us that maybe because of the snow or something my mother
was not well and could not return.

Fleeing From an Abusive Partner or Family Conflict

Some participants explained the parent's departure as caused by an abusive relationship with a spouse or partner. In other cases, conflict between the parents and their family of origin caused them to leave. Compared to being forced to leave because of an external enemy (such as war or poverty), fleeing from conflict within the family or marriage was not as heroic or as easy for the participants to internalize or come to terms with. Fleeing from an abusive relationship or a broken heart presented a much greater source of conflict and anxiety for these children because suddenly, the enemy was inside the family, and in most cases, among people the children wanted to love and be close to. This implied that instead of the family providing protection and security against outside danger, it had to fold itself in and fight against internal threat. The children now found themselves forced to take sides and choose between family members, which represented an immense source of conflict.

In Luis's case, his father's drinking forced his mother to leave her husband. Although he did not say that his father was being abusive, he hinted that when the father came home drunk, he bothered the children and did not allow his mother to sleep.

> [My parents] were married for several years. Afterwards, they separated because of his addiction... one year after I was born they separated. Because... he was like, a drunk, and he did not know what he was doing. He used to bother us, and wouldn't let her [my mother] sleep. And he didn't work. So, she decided to leave him. But it was not easy for her because she was thinking about us, that we would not have the love of a father, and of her, because she was also going to leave [to the U.S.] soon.

Luis's strategy was to make the father's alcoholism the external enemy. This split helped him protect this internal representation of the father as good, and blame the alcoholic father for the family problems. He seems to excuse the father's behavior by saying that he was a drunk and therefore did not know what he was doing. Yet, the absence of a strong, external cause for the mother's departure cast doubts on Luis's sense of self as loveable, "And a person then, had thoughts... that it was only because she didn't want him, she didn't want him, that the mother had left me with others, and all that... That is why. But now I understand why she... yes, now that I grew up..." Luis alternates between using the first person and an abstract third person, as if trying to remove himself emotionally from the situation of abandonment. This could also suggest his effort to normalize covert feelings of resentment towards his mother by implying that "one'" (i.e., anybody in his place) would feel rejected under those circumstances.

In Rita's case, her mother could not deal with the pressure of living with a husband who was not accepted by her family. In addition, there was much disagreement between Rita's mother and her brothers about inheritance and property, which led to the mother being eventually disowned.

> My mother had everything, but then there was a problem. It seems that my uncle, the youngest one, he told my grandmother to give nothing to my mother. So, my grandma told my mom to sell the restaurant and my mom obeyed her. And my uncle told my grandma not to give my mother her share of the inheritance, so my mother decided to come and... This was the problem. So this is why I did not think about it [the mother's motives to leave]. Because she had everything, the only thing was that they did not support her... and that is why I could not get it in my head.

If for Luis the cause of the parent's separation was an external factor (alcohol abuse), in Rita case the parent's separation was caused by disagreements within the family. Rita felt much shame around the mother's status of single parent, and at a loss as to why the grandmother had such immense dislike for the father. Rita hinted that there were serious fights between the parents, and that her mother's second husband was violent towards the mother up to the time that Rita and her sister arrived in the U.S.

> My grandma and my father did not get along... because my mom, my grandma did not approve of my mother being with my father. So, they did not get along. I only knew that my

grandma hated my father. This was in part why my mother and my father could not be together. This was one reason... so, of course, that made me suffer. But then I got used to it.

When I asked Carla what she thought made her mother leave El Salvador, she started by talking about marital problems between the parents. But then, Carla quickly moved to the family's lack of resources, explaining that even food was becoming unavailable. She concluded this was ultimately what made the mother immigrate. It could be that Carla was trying to defend herself by conceptualizing the mother's departure as a sacrifice caused by external enemies rather than by family discord.

Oh, I believe that basically my dad [was the reason my mother left]. My dad told my mom, "I want that the children be with my family [parents]." And she told him, "no". And so, my father basically did not want my mother. And that is when she said, " no, then I will go [to the U.S.]." Because there was a time, a time when I believe she couldn't even buy food. Do you know tortillas? That was all there was. It was terrible. So my mother saw the situation and ... I mean, it was terrible. So I believe this was one of the reasons. For us and for my family.

They Are Working Hard for Us

The second factor that influenced how the children internalized the parent's immigration as abandonment or sacrifice was associated with the parents' dependability in providing and contacting the children while they were apart. Periodic contact through phone calls, letters, presents, and money was essential to validate the participants' belief that the parents left for the benefit of the children. Moreover, if influential adults, such as surrogate parents and caretakers, reinforced the children's perception of sacrifice, and if the community supported and normalized the parents' decision, it was easier for the children not to feel abandoned during the period of separation.

A Better Life:

Some children had concrete experiences and recollections of how much better life became once the parent was in the U.S. a while. For some, shacks were replaced with brick homes. For others, the houses became larger, or better furnished. Food, clothes, and school materials were now available, and such objects became material proof and constant reminders that the parents were in fact working for the children's sake. Those objects and presents also functioned as a continued emotional link between the child and the absent parent: a modified version of transitional objects (10).

Alex, for example, saw that the life of his family improved after his father and two uncles came to the U.S.; "... we started getting new stuff, like, new furniture, new beds, better clothes, better shoes from here, and we actually... we started eating better." Alex also found it easier to protect himself from the sarcasm of classmates because he often had something to show his friends as proof that the parents cared for him. Finally, his parents were married and living together in the U.S.

> Yes, they [friends] knew [that my parents were in the U.S.], so they did not make fun of us because ... when sometimes they ask you, "Where are your parents at?", so we told them, "They are right there in the United States", and when they asked, "What are they doing there?" "Ok, they are working hard for us, see? Look at those new shoes they sent. They bought it for us, they sent to us, so we know they are working hard for us."

Very much like Alex, Luis was able to justify the mother's absence and to prove that she cared about him by showing his friends the shoes and clothes she sent periodically. "When my friends saw me, they noticed my shoes and [the fact] that I was well dressed, and they'd say 'Well, you look good', and [I replied] 'She still writes to me and sends me money...'. There was always a good dialogue". One cannot help but notice that Luis used the expression "She <u>still</u> writes to me and sends me money", as if expecting that, after a while, his mother would no longer remember him, keep in contact, or provide for his needs.

For other participants, their lack of comments on how the mother sent them money and presents also seemed significant. Rita and Suzana, for example, did not once mention the mother contacting them or sending them money and presents. Rita says that she knows her mother now cares for her because she makes sure that Rita has the school materials she needs, for example. In contrast, Rut talked about how while she was in the care of her aunt and uncle, they always made sure to treat her like their own children. She illustrated her point by telling me that they always bought her the same things they got for their own children. For Suzana, the fact that her uncle gave her what she wanted meant that he loved her like his own children,

> My uncle, every month, every weekend, when he had money... so I said, "I want, I want this", [and] my uncle would go get it. My uncle has been more of a father to me than to his own kids. And you can ask anybody who knows him; they know. "Oh yes, he used to buy her dresses, he used to spoil this little girl.

... and she then continued by saying that she would do anything to help that uncle.

> And now that he is going through some hard problems, that is the person who I am most willingly, pleasantly - and I don't expect nothing from God in return -, who I would love to help... and nobody has to force me to do it. That is a person who I don't even have to think twice to help."

However, at times it was difficult for these children to get their emotional needs met through material objects. In most cases, they did not dare to recognize even to themselves their mixed feelings about the parents' departure. Suzana, for example, resented the pressure she felt from her caretakers to constantly present herself as grateful of her mother's efforts.

> I [thought], "don't tell me about it anymore", you know? Because, every time, [my grandmother would say], "your mom loves you, your mom this... *"But I wouldn't see it* ! Because, just because she used to send money! Well, that

means nothing to me. I was, I mean ... I was 5, 6 years old!
What does money meant to me? I didn't care! I was getting
everything I wanted, but I didn't know it was because of her.
And my aunt and my uncles were working. Money... I was
like, I was like, looking for love, you know? Even though I
had it, but I wanted it from my mom... It was like, I wanted
all those three people who were giving me [love], all of those
people, *plus her* to give me love.

Even for participants such as Luis, who struggled to hold on to a
unidimensional, positive view of the mother's decision to immigrate,
there was always the nagging feeling that presents and money were just
not enough at times.

No, I felt happy for her, because she came here to bring ... she
made a great effort to build the house, to bring us over ... my
older brother, and now we are here. Always helping us, always
sending money, and all... always a gift, sending things, and
all... But we always missed the love of a mother, because you
can't buy love with money and things. Because I missed
talking to her, being with her and all that.

Caretakers as Keepers of Memories

Caretakers not only took care of the children during the period of
separation, but also had the very important task of preserving the image
of the absent parent as caring and committed to the children. The
messages, beliefs, and behaviors of caretakers during the separation
helped these children process and integrate their experience. Alex's
grandmother, for example, was consistent and quite creative in
conveying to the children that their parents were in the U.S. "working
hard for them". On the days that his parents sent them money, she took
Alex and his sisters out to eat. This made a strong impression on Alex,
bringing together the concepts of sacrifice, celebration, special
occasion, and food - a metaphor for love and nurturance, and often
mentioned by the participants.

Hum... When my dad usually send money for us, and my mom [actually, his grandmother], she always told us, "this is for you; your dad and your mom are working hard for you, so you gotta study hard for them too." And she usually, when always she get like, the money they send, she would go buy some ... like chicken made already; like ... she didn't cook that day. She always got the money, we all six would go to eat in a restaurant. So she was always teaching us how ... how we are supposed to love our parents because they were working hard for us, so that when we get the money, we are supposed to thank them, give a prayer to them, because they worked so hard for us.... That is what I remember.

Alex repeats the same phrase so many times that the reader gets the feeling that he was recreating the voice of the grandmother, which by now has been incorporated as his own voice. Also of note is that Alex, like most participants, often referred to the caretaker as mother or father. This could symbolize their confusion about who they where supposed to internalize as their parent.

It is interesting to observe how some participants internalized the caretakers' voice as their own, as they tried to explain to themselves why the parents were not with them. In a brief account, we heard Alex tell his friends that his parents were in the U.S. "working hard for us". A little later in the interview, Alex used the exact same expression to describe the grandmother's words as she explained to him why his parents left to the U.S. Of course, the order is most likely reversed: The grandmother's voice became his own voice as he tried to build a coherent schema around the parents' prolonged absence. This process probably explains my instinctual reaction to many of these interviews: I often had the feeling that what I was in fact hearing was the caretaker's voice, although spoken throughout the child in front of me. Sometimes I wondered, where did these children's own voices go.

In Luis's account, his words give the reader the feeling that the grandmother's explanations and his own blend together, and that his voice is solely the parroting of what he heard the grandmother often say. It could be that the children were responding to their need to construct a tightly closed reality as a way to protect their internal representation of the absent parent as committed, sacrificing, and benign.

Yes, she [grandmother] talked to us, explained and told us
things about her [mother] so that we would never feel
rejection towards her, and so that we would never forget her,
because she came to this country because of us. That is why
she explained several things. What my grandmother said was
that she came to this country for a better future for us and that
we had to thank her for what she is doing because it was... it
was not easy for her to come to this country; be far from us....
That my brothers and I had to respect her and also love her.
That it is because of her that we are now in this country.

Some children seemed to have most of the ideal factors in place to
help them internalize the parent's immigration as a sacrifice. Alex, for
example, had one caring and appropriate caretaker during the entire
period of separation: his paternal grandmother, whom he remembers as
loving and protective. The parents left because of poverty. The parents
were married and living together in the U.S. Alex and his siblings lived
together during the separation from his parents. Alex's parents were
dependable in providing for the children during the years of separation,
and he knew other children who experienced the same circumstances.
Yet, there was still the lingering feeling of being abandoned and the
unspoken anger and resentment towards the parents. Those unspoken
feelings often surfaced during fights, when emotions could not be
contained. This becomes clear in one of Alex's interview segments:

...we didn't do that stuff [doing chores], I am telling you. I
was the spoiled baby in the house and my dad didn't like that
...and I didn't respect my dad. It was hard because when he
started bossing us, like many parents, we usually didn't
answer them; we were rude. "You are not our friend, you
weren't there for us". We usually told them a lot of stupid
stuff. He wasn't there for Christmas, for our birthday, so "why
are you coming to boss us right now? We are old now, you
know?" My dad [would] get mad.... I remember one day
when my dad hit me because I answer him real rude ... I was
stupid, and my mom usually cry because ... when usually we
answer her real rude, she usually cried.

For Suzana, feeling unable to talk openly about her doubts and prohibited to ask questions contributed to her feelings of self-doubt, confusion, and resentment.

> *Author*: So, when you were a child, what kind of stories did you tell yourself about the reason why your mother came to the United States?
>
> *Suzana*: Like, Ok … They would tell me one thing, and I would think another thing.
>
> *Author*: What would you think?
>
> *Suzana*: I thought that maybe it was… at first I used to think, "yeah, maybe because there was no money and everything", but then, after a time, I was like "she probably didn't love me … she probably didn't want to be with me", you know? They would be like, "She is not here", and I would be like, why? "Because she went to raise the money for us", and I would say that sometimes, but sometimes I didn't mean that, sometimes I didn't know what to think! Because sometimes my cousins, I know they used to play, but, you know, you as a little boy, you as a little girl . . . you don't think that, and my cousins would say, "you know, your mom left you because she didn't love you!" So, then my grandma, she wouldn't like that, and she would be like, "Don't be telling her that! That is not true", you know? Because my grandma knew that when someone used to tell me things, they used to get me thinking.

It seems that one of the caretaker's unspoken functions was that of keeper of the image and memory of the absent parent as self-sacrificing and committed to the family. Such task was unquestionably important, and caretakers were, for the most part, well intended. However, in that process, they may have inadvertently sent less desirable messages to those children. Sometimes overtly, other times covertly, those adults often urged the children to suppress all feelings and expression of anger and resentment towards the absent parent.

There seems to be mainly three harmful messages that these children got from their caretakers during the separation. First, children feared that any feelings of grief, loss, or resentment towards the absent parent or parents might be interpreted as selfishness and ingratitude for the parents' sacrifice. Second, by putting on a brave face and not showing their sadness, the children were in fact trying to protect the parents from experiencing their sadness and frustration for having to leave the family. If all involved pretend that nobody is really hurting, then it becomes easier to carry on the illusion that in fact nobody is suffering. In addition, children and parents had their roles reversed, with the children being placed in the position of emotional caretakers of the parents. Third, the relationship between parent and child often had a give-and-take, business quality to it. Caretakers told the children they had to study hard, behave well, respect, and love their parents because the parents were in the U.S. for their sake, so that the children could have a better life; so that they could have a better future. The children were to thank and pray for the parents each time they sent them money. Sadly, children were robbed not only of the day-to-day company of the parent, but also of the essential experience of being loved and loving unconditionally. The question then remains: Were such messages protective factors or were they one more source of stress and conflict for these children? If protective, under what circumstances?

INTERNAL WORKING MODEL OF SELF

In the second research question I inquired about the impact of the prolonged separation and the participants' interpretation of that event as abandonment or sacrifice on their representational model (or internal working model) of self. The third research question was concerned with the impact of the separation on the participants' internal working model of others. Although questions 2 and 3 are closely related and often overlap, I will try as much as possible to treat them separately in this chapter.

Attachment styles are directly influenced by internal working models of self and others. People with a secure attachment style often see themselves (or have a representational model of self) as worthy of love and protection. They also trust that caretakers and other adults will be willing and able to meet their emotional needs (internal working model of others). On the other hand, children with insecure attachment styles often experience significant adults and caretakers as unreliable, unable, or unwilling to provide the nurturance and protection they need.

Consequently, they will be more likely to internalize a concept of self as undeserving of love and protection from others.

It was not the purpose of this study to classify the attachment style of each participant. However, it was a purpose of this project to better understand the impact and perception of the separation in the general attachment patterns of the participants through the exploration of the participants' internal working model of self and others. How participants saw themselves, how they conceptualized the concepts of feeling loved, and their hopes for the future could indicate their preferred patterns of attachment. Of the coding categories identified in the interviews, the ones that most closely related to the impact of the separation on the participants' internal working model of self are shown in Table 5.

Table 5. Coding categories: Internal Working Models of Self

FREE NODES	TREE NODES		
	DAMAGED GOODS	HEROES	LOVE
Competency	Culture as damaged	Culture as hero	Spoiled
Career			Playing
School	Self as damaged	Self as hero	Punishment
Divided Loyalties			Respect
Role Reversal	Life as damaged	Life as hero	Talking
Guilt			Food
Shame			

The Many Facets of Love

Participants talked about being loved by using examples of behaviors and through metaphors. As I looked at the way participants described how they felt in relation to their parents and how they related to their caretakers, some subcategories emerged. Love was synonymous with being nourished and fed, with playing, joking, talking, and respecting the parental figure. Most participants volunteered memories of caretakers cooking for them, and food was mentioned in all interviews, usually associated with feelings of being loved and cared for. Parents demonstrated their love by sending money and presents to the participants. Whereas most children mentioned how they were able to talk and play with their caretakers, when referring to their parents, they talked about respect and authority. Finally, many children equated being loved with being spoiled.

Spoiled or Special?
The concept of being spoiled implied two conflicting messages. On the one hand, it implied that the participants saw themselves as special and therefore deserving of having all of their needs and wishes fulfilled. On the other hand, it also implied that they were getting more than they deserved, and therefore, that they were being damaged (or spoiled) in some way. An interesting phenomenon seemed to occur. For every interview segment coded as "spoiled" or "damaged goods" with its subcategories ("parent as damaged", "self as damaged", or "family as damaged"), the interview segment that followed was usually coded using one of the "hero" subcategories (such as "parent as hero", "self as hero", and "family as hero"). I believe that this pattern of thinking illustrates these children's internal strategy to protect their ego and their self-image as loveable, as well as to protect the image of their parents as able to give them the love and protection they needed. The participants had to deal with two discordant concepts of self simultaneously: That they were special, and therefore deserving of the parent's sacrifice, but also that they were spoiled, and therefore not deserving of anybody's love and affection. This gave these children a sense of great importance and in some cases, a sense of entitlement. Such inflated sense of self seemed to compensate their feelings of rejection and inadequacy. Finally, some participants seemed to be making a great effort to convince me that, although they had not been raised by their parents, they had been well treated and loved during their early years.

Luis feared that his mother's absence might reflect on him and be interpreted as his being unworthy of her love.

No, and, and, I almost did not like to talk [about my mother] at school because it looked really bad to be separated from my mother, and all .... Yeah, one feels ugly because the others had their parents with them, and all... they went out with the kids... And in contrast, if one was not, was not with them, one felt very ugly... One does not feel like others.

It is interesting to note how Luis changes from present to past and back to present tense and how he goes back and forth between first and third person. This could suggest his effort to create some distance between him and his account, making it less personal, and therefore less threatening to his image of self. Luis then follows this segment with the explanation of how other students used to talk about their mothers cooking for them and taking them out.

Yes, they [my friends] always said that "Oh, because my mom cooks for me, dresses me up", and all that... and they and their mother would go out .... Oh, they would go to the beach, and we, on the other hand, we almost did not leave the house because my grandma, she almost didn't like to go out.

Alex described with much enthusiasm the time his grandmother came for a three-month visit. During that time, he and his sisters seemed to be a priority in the grandmother's daily activities. Their mother, on the other hand, had to divide her energy between work and family.

We wake up at 5:45. It is kind of early, and my grandma is always, wake up to make us coffee or tea ... She always, like ... It is nice for us, she doesn't let us go out if we did not drink that coffee or tea, or milk. See? It is kind of spoil, you know? And after we come back from school, our food always is ready at the table, and we start eating right away. And it is usually, like, when I go to work, she always wakes up at 5:45, and makes us the coffee and breakfast. When I go to work, and she always asks me if I've got money for lunch and if not, she always makes us some sandwich, some salad ... She ... I feel nice when she is here. And the only thing, she made my mom lazy because she did the whole work, and my mom doesn't do it...

Alex equated being fed (nurtured) with being loved, and feared that the mother would not become nurturing because she had no need to; his grandmother did everything for him and his sisters. Suzana also got the message that she was spoiled because her mother was working in the U.S. so that Suzana could live comfortably in a four-bedroom house, as we saw earlier in this chapter. At other times, Suzana was told that her grandmother spoiled her with too much love.

> And when I used to talk to her [to the mother, over the telephone] I used to be like, "hi mummy, I love you." . . . I hated her, but I always felt that ... you know? And the thing that made it worse was when I came here and she treated me different than my aunt and my grandma. Because what they did, I could say they spoiled me, because anything I wanted, if they could they would get it for me.

Suzana seems confused about whether she deserved to be loved. The caretakers treated her well but her own mother seemed very critical and non-accepting of her. Other participants voiced similar feelings of confusion and little understanding about how they should be treated. It almost seems that, somewhere along the way, those children got the implicit (and sometimes explicit) message that they did not deserve to be loved and treated well.

Playing, Talking, and Respect:
Alex equated playing and talking with having a close and trusting relationship, and said that such were the characteristics of his interactions with his grandmother and father. His relationship with his mother, however, was defined by respect, formalities, hierarchy, and appropriate manners. There was also a sense of hurt, confusion, and doubt, as he tried to explain and justify his mother's personality and behaviors toward her children.

I can play with my grandmother the same as with my dad. I can play jokes.... It depends [on] what kind of joke you do with them, you know? It is not like that with my mom. I don't understand my mom because that is her opinion, so we respect that. . . . My mom, I respect her, but she doesn't show you that love like other moms. She doesn't kiss you, you know? She doesn't like that. She doesn't like to spoil their childrens; she only.... when we need to talk to her, we talk to her and she does it for us. That is the way, you know what I am saying? Because my grandma, she spoils when she comes. She usually comes and gives us a kiss. The same with my dad. When he comes from work, and we are sleeping, he goes to our room and gives us a kiss. Not my mom. She goes to our room, checks us out, and get out. That is all. So my mom doesn't spoil. But that is the way she was raised, so there is nothing we can do about it. We don't understand. I don't understand my mom.

For Rita, the conversations with her mother must be limited to the casual, day-to-day chatting, as Rita believes that her mother would not understand her if she were to talk about how she really feels.

Yes, because I can talk to my mother about the daily things that happen to me, because they are daily things. Things that happen in school, and all that... But if I were to tell her how I feel inside, we would not get along ... we would not get along.

Similarly, Jorge equated trust and the ability to talk to his mother with being loved. In his case, however, he felt he could trust his mother with his feelings. "I have, I don't know ... I don't know how to explain, but I trust her, I trust her with my things ... we talk. Because she helps me if I have some problem. Like that."

Some participants, particularly the older ones, seemed to make a clear effort to integrate the image and concept of the parents in a more balanced, less polarized fashion. In several occasions, soon after criticizing the parent, these adolescents quickly tried to justify and defend the parent's behavior. This correction could in fact indicate that they were starting to tolerate the image of the parent as "less than perfect"; a parent different from what they needed or wished for, but

nonetheless a reality they knew they had to make peace with. Alex, for
example, talked about how disengaged and disaffectionate his mother
could be at times, only to justify and protect her behavior in his
following statement, saying that in fact she was doing the best she can.

> [T]hat is the way she [my mother] is... She cannot change
> it... There is nothing we can do about it. But she loves us.
> She really loves us. When I ask her, I need to... I need
> somebody to make some food to take to school, and she came
> from work, she was so tired, I asked her to do it, and she did it
> and she went to bed around 12 o'clock. That shows some love.
> That is an example.

Parents' Marital Status

All participants seemed to give much importance to the parents' marital
status. They saw marital separation and having a child out of wedlock
as shameful and as a reflection on their own self-worth. They felt
inadequate and less valuable compared to their peers. For those whose
parents were married and together, there was an unspoken pride. In
addition, those with unmarried mothers felt more anxious and insecure
about the immigration situation. Much like Luis, they feared that if the
mother or father found a new partner in the U.S. and started a new
family here, there was a greater chance that they would forget the
children left south of the border. As Luis explained to me, "Yes,
because some people say that when one comes to this country, she
forgets about the children, and all that, and gets married to someone
else and does not communicate with the children, with the family."

For Rita, there was the shame of being the daughter of a single
mother and the sadness around the father's lack of involvement with his
daughters.

> And yes, I suffered a lot because there were times when all my
> friends at school, they lived with their mother and father.
> Because yes, in Latin America, if you don't have a father, you
> feel rejected, I don't know. But yes, the parents are always
> together, I mean ... if you have a stepfather or a stepmother,

the others see you as different, because your parents are not together... So I did not have my father nor my mother, but instead I lived with my uncles. And everybody talked about their mothers, and with my girlfriends, I didn't know what to talk about because I was not living with my mother. So, yeah, this was hard for me, yeah.

In addition to the shame and sadness, Rita felt much anger and distrust because of the repeated lies and secrecy that characterized the mother's relationship with her. It wasn't until Rita arrived in the U.S., for example, that she learned that her mother had married four years earlier. To make matters worse, the mother blamed Rita's favorite aunt for failing her "obligation" to tell Rita about the marriage.

Absence of Remarriages and Other Children:
Conversely, if the parents were married and together in the U.S., the children felt safer about the possibility of being reunited to them in the future. Alex had the reassurance of the grandmother that his parents were together in the U.S., working hard for the children. Jorge also talked about the parent's being together as a factor that made him feel more secure and loved during the years they lived apart. For Isabela, while the father was alive, there were plans for him and the children to again live as a family. However, the death of her father dampened the family's plans to reunite "They wanted that my father come here and that the whole family reunite again, here, but we couldn't because the thieves killed my father at his work."

Trusting Oneself and Competency

As I looked at the data, the issue of participants' sense of competency and trust in their own abilities to negotiate the world seemed mostly related to two different aspects of their self image. Participants talked about their educational goals and dreams for future careers, and for the most part, they seemed to think of themselves as able to learn and to ultimately achieve their professional objectives. On the other hand, participants talked with much less confidence about their ability to fulfil their future roles as spouses and parents. These two distinct "areas of functioning" seemed unrelated and independent from each other, particularly among the females interviewed for this project.

School and Career:
Most participants considered school and career a priority. They
reported they took school seriously, and for the most part, they seemed
to have goals and ambition for their future. This could indicate a
healthy trust in their abilities and a secure and hopeful sense about their
future. It could also suggest that they have internalized a strong sense
of obligation to succeed as their repayment to the parents for all the
sacrifices they made. In some cases, they explicitly verbalized such
thinking. As the data indicate earlier in this chapter, Alex, Carla,
Isabela, and Luis justified the parent's immigration as their way to
secure a better education and therefore a better future for the children.
However, although they took school seriously, many of them did quite
poorly academically. Except for Rita and Carla, all other participants
had below average grades. Alex's explanation that he did not work hard
in school because he did not pay for it seemed related to the idea that
doing well in school was the way these children could make a
restitution to the parent for his or her dedication to the family. Alex
said that he now took school seriously, but that this wasn't the case
when he lived in Guatemala.

> ... when we went to school with my cousins in Guatemala, we
> didn't care about school. We went to a private high school, we
> spent like $100 for each month for private school. So we
> didn't care. I remember I didn't care about school.... Perhaps
> because we didn't earn that money for school so we thought it
> was easy.

Carla, on the other hand, struggled with the thought that she may
not ever be able to learn English. She even referred to her
determination to continue trying as a *sacrifice* she would make to
compensate for the fact that her parents did not graduate from high
school – due to her mother's pregnancy with Carla, as a matter or fact.

> ... we were in an ESL program, which is a program to learn
> English, and I said, "no, I will never succeed." And I had to
> overcome, because none of my parents, my father and my

mother, neither of them could graduate. So I decided to make
a sacrifice...

For Rita and Isabela, for example, competency, mastery, and the
ability to negotiate successfully with the outside world were associated
with having a supportive father. Rita did well in school, and yet she
longed for the help of her father, "Maybe I would have had more help
when I was little and did not understand the lessons; maybe my father
would have helped me". Isabela's memories of her father were for the
most part related to school and learning.

Because we always had the image of my father as being very
intelligent, because he always made us read, read a lot, and he
told us stories. I talked about the stories he told us at school.
He made us study orthography a lot, and always talked about
it, but...

All participants had a fairly clear idea of what profession they
would like to pursue. With the exception of Rita, all female
interviewees were drawn to the helping professions, such as nursing
and psychology. Jorge had a realistic and practical plan of being a
skilled laborer and Alex had dreams of owning a construction
company. Luis and Rita wanted to work in the technology field. I was
surprised to see that even the younger children had given some thought
to their future profession and goals. After all, many of them were
identified through a school-based program for teenagers identified as
being at-risk for dropping out of school.

Marriage and Children:
As they talked about school and career, all participants presented as
confident and hopeful for their future. However, the thought of having
a spouse and children seemed to overwhelm most of them, particularly
the teenage girls. They seemed to see themselves as unable to carry on
the task of raising a family, and they feared they would lack money,
time, and emotional resources. Maybe they were projecting onto
themselves their unspoken or unidentified feelings of abandonment and
their view of the parents as inadequate and unable to provide for their
emotional and material needs. On the other hand, their perception was
firmly based on reality. After all, most of them had a first-hand

experience of seeing their parents struggle to accommodate work and family, with work invariably getting the best of them. Finally, some participants mentioned how difficult it would be to keep their children away from getting involved in crime or from joining gangs. Here too, they might be expressing doubts about their own ability to resist the constant pressure and desire to join gangs.

As I analyzed the data, a quite well-defined pattern around the issue of having a family and raising children seemed to emerge. Carla, Rita, and Suzana were among those who thought that raising a family would be an overwhelming and risky business. On the other hand, Alex, Jorge, and Luis seemed to welcome the idea of having a wife and children. The gender line seemed evident. Isabela's perception was unique because she was dealing not with the thought, but rather with the reality of child-rearing. Carla reported,

> Yes, see… maybe people say I am crazy and all that, but to have children in the United States is not an option. You should have a lot of money to raise the children, or not to have them. You need to really know how to take care of a child, you need to be patient when the child cries at 2 o'clock in the morning… and see, when you have a child you need to stay with that 24/ 7. You know what I mean? And these people need to go to work, and they have a babysitter. I wouldn't like that… And basically, they are not the ones to have a problem. The child is born to stay next to the mother, and if not that, the babysitter is abusing the child, and you know you will never gonna be fine . . . And you must pay for Medicaid, and if it gets sick … I mean, I love children, but a family? No. I was like, 'no way'. And then, when it gets to high school, what happens to this child? [He] is gonna be maybe a gang member, you know? And you don't know how to control it … because I don't feel I am strong enough to control a child.

Rita believed that a career would be her insurance against the inevitable romantic disappointments she would encounter;

If, for example, if something happens to me, at least I have my career. For example, if I, for example, if I fell in love, and, and, and all fell apart in my relationship, I know that I have my career and that I can go on."

Suzana did not sound very enthusiastic when asked if she planned to get married or have children. She felt she was too young to commit to a marriage and a to family; a fair appraisal at her age. Earlier in the interview, however, Suzana volunteered that although she loved children, she felt she would not have the resources needed to raise a healthy and happy child in the U.S. In fact, all participants talked about how little time people have for their families due to demands from jobs, and some became angry and resentful when talking about how children are mostly raised by babysitters.

In contrast to the female interviewees, all the males interviewed for this project said that wife and children would play an important role in their future. Alex wanted to be financially successful before he settled down and got married. Considering his father's lack of financial stability and Alex's dismay to discover he had a half-brother about his age, his statement might reflect his desire to repair the father's shortcomings.

I prefer to make my own future, buy my own house, two cars, live by myself, live the life, enjoy the life first, then get married at 27, 28. Before that, I have to make myself and my wife a future. Then, my children, I have to have a lot of toys for them, you know? Save some money to take vacation, save some money, not work so hard .... Then I am gonna work first, real hard, to make my own stuff, then make my family stuff ... Then find a wife...My hope is, if you bring a baby to the world, you have to help your baby to have anything it needs, you know? So I got to make my own future, then my family future... and help my parents too. I say: family first.

Alex's sense of obligation to his parents seems as strong as his plans to be a reliable provider to his future family. Such cultural values are certainly congruent with both the literature and with my personal experience in working with Latino families. In fact, Alex seemed to feel the need to further explore this particular need later on in the interview. The theme of his second sand tray is in fact about the farm in Guatemala he would buy for his parents, so that *they* could have a better future (Please refer to Appendix B for a photo of Alex's sand tray number two).

> *Author*: Can you tell me a little bit about this house and this part of the tray, with the house, three people and the boat?
> *Alex*: It is going to be the future of my parents, and I think, I want to buy them a house, and if they want to go back to Guatemala .... You see, my mom was used to having a lot of money and a farm. This is gonna be a little restaurant and my mom is going to cook...
> *Author*: So they are going to have a little restaurant in the countryside, in a farm ... And those 2 figures, are they your mom and dad? Is that what these are?
> *Alex*: Yeah.
> *Author*: And who is that here?
> *Alex*: Somebody to help my mom .... So, my mom want to put a restaurant, and me and my sister will help. They want to go back to Guatemala, so.... Their work is killing them, you know? So we got to stop being selfish. My mom and my dad want to have a house outside of the city, and they could have cows for the meat for the restaurant...
> *Author*. Oh, so they could raise their cows, and plant their own vegetables. Well, that is an interesting idea. Do you want to give a title to your tray?
> *Alex*: We can call it "Future of my parents". I hope they will be happy.

The dialogue above is representative of Alex's sense of loyalty and of his internal need to protect his parents. It is also interesting to note how Alex set up a scenario where his mother was forced to cook (to nourish him?). Alex stated earlier of how gratifying it was for him to come home to find that the meal prepared by his grandmother was waiting for them on the table. In the same breath he characterized his mother as too busy to cook for them. This could suggest an internal desire to create the right conditions to force his mother and father to nurture their children.

Luis also joined Alex in his desire to help his mother before looking for a wife. When asked if he thought of someday getting married or having babies, he answered,

> Yes, but later ... Right now, I am not thinking about it .... I thought about it, but later, when I already have my career, after I become a professional, and all that... study, and give the money to my mother, for about three or four years, and then look for a wife.

And when asked about his plans for the future, Jorge responded in his characteristic monosyllabic style, "I want to get married." Despite further prompting, I was not able to get much information beyond stereotypical statements.

Children interviewed for this project seemed to define love somewhat differently based on whom they were close to in the early years of development. Authority, hierarchy, and respect were mostly mentioned when talking about the absent parent, whereas trust, playfulness, and unconditional love seemed to define the relationship of the children with caretakers who were present for the first 6 or 7 years of the child's development. Children from intact families felt a greater sense of self worth and protection, while children of single or divorced parents felt that there was something inherently defective about themselves or their parents. Besides feeling ashamed about their status they were also anxious about their role in the family. All children seemed to give much importance to their future careers. This could be related to the message sent by the parents that they had come to the U.S. so that the children could have a better future. By taking school and career seriously, the children would both pay the parents back for their sacrifice and show them that they were worthy of the parents' efforts. Some of them seemed to feel obligated to pay the parents back by taking care of them even before starting their own family. Finally, whereas the males interviewed were attracted by the idea of raising a family, females felt anxious about becoming wives and mothers. They seemed to see those tasks as either not "worth of the trouble" or see themselves as unprepared for the role. Considering that, in Latino culture, nurturance is almost exclusively a woman's responsibility, the anxiety of these young ladies is understandable. For girls, a history of separation may have had an impact on how they perceived their own ability to become caretakers.

INTERNAL WORKING MODELS OF OTHERS

As mentioned earlier in this chapter, the third research question addressed the impact of prolonged separation and its interpretation as abandonment or sacrifice on the participants' representational model (or internal working model) of others. Were children separated from parents more likely to see others as unreliable or unable to provide for their need of love and protection? How could the negative impact of separation be minimized? Which behaviors and circumstances facilitated the view of adults as dependable? Which ones hindered that process? Table 6 displays the coding categories that seemed most relevant in the answer to these questions.

Table 6. Coding categories: Internal Working Models of Others

FREE NODES	TREE NODES		
	DAMAGED GOODS	HEROES	LOVE
Divided Loyalties	Culture as damaged	Culture as hero	Respect
Sibling bonding			Talking
Trauma	Parents as damaged	Parents as heroes	Playing
War			Going out
Losses	Life as damaged	Life as hero	Punishment

Explanations

Few of the participants were adequately informed of the parents' decision to leave. Even fewer felt they had a voice in their parents' decision. In fact, many of them did not even have a chance to say goodbye to the parents before their departure, and some children believed for many years that the parent was in a city nearby and would return soon. This seemed to add to the participants' perception that adults could not be trusted.

Saying Goodbye:
Parents often left without saying goodbye or explaining to the children why they were leaving until much later, in some cases, until years later. This seemed to place an extra burden on the children and to contribute to their view of adults as unreliable and untrustworthy. Participants talked about their stress following the parents' disappearance, and the attempts of the caretakers to appease them by telling lies or by continuing the vow of silence around the parents' absence.

To this day Carla feels much sadness and anger around the family's silence and lies surrounding the mother's immigration. As she talked about her memories, she could not contain her tears. As Carla cried, she recreated in great detail the conversation with her uncle. That conversation was the first time that an adult told Carla the truth about the mother's whereabouts and the circumstances of her departure. By that time it had been two years since her mother had disappeared from her Carla's life.

> I think that, think that ... I had many ... [crying]... Because I was seven... and I would tell myself, "but why did she leave? And I did not even see her ... she didn't give me a kiss". And he [uncle] said, "she came to say goodbye but you were asleep and she did not want to wake you up .... Because if we woke you up she would not leave." When he said that, my uncle, I said, "she herself was very sad because she wanted to takes us with her. She wanted to take us, it did not matter how, but she wanted to take us too." [uncle] "And you were asleep, it was 4 or 5 o'clock in the morning, you were asleep and she told us that if you woke up she would not be able to leave. And so, she left." Seven years ... it was a long time.

In this passage one almost gets the impression that the message is that the child is responsible for the mother failing to say goodbye. Because the adult cannot bear her sadness and say goodbye, then the child has to, by herself, come to terms with this new reality. In the way that Carla described the event, roles are reversed, and the child is made responsible for the parent's action. Furthermore, the child is the one expected to contain the anxiety, grief, and distress of the parent.

Grandparents, on the other hand, were able to say proper good-byes. Maybe because the children were older by the time they left to the U.S., the family thought they now would be able to understand what was happening and therefore it would be appropriate to say farewell. In these circumstances, both parties had the opportunity to experience the separation in a less destructive manner and get a healthier sense of closure and purpose. In a ritual that lasted over a month before his departure, Luis and his grandmother spent a lot of time together, talking and going for special outings together. They seemed to be processing and grieving the upcoming loss, a process that allowed them to fully experience the transition. In addition, because most of these children expected to join the parents in the U.S. at some point, they had been prepared for the departure and separation from their grandparents for many years.

> We had one month after she [grandmother] told us, and we went out with her and all that, so that we would not feel the separation so strongly… We went out and spent time talking to her, and she gave us advice and told us to take care of my mother; that we take care of her and that we not be mean to her, you know? Because she came to this country to give us a better future, and that not everybody does that for their children. To give the children away and come to a country alone … that was her advice.

Rita's mother not only failed to say goodbye, but also kept telling her that she would soon return. Such behavior contributed to Rita's feeling in a continuous roller coaster of hope followed by disappointment. The mother's handling of the situation made the separation even more painful for Rita. In addition, trusting adults and relying on them for support became almost impossible, and at the end, Rita had only herself to rely on.

For the first days that she left, oh ... I cried because, I mean, I couldn't understand what was going on. But, she had a reason to leave, because she had some problems, and that is why she left. So, she would talk to me and I would ask when she was going to come back, and she would tell me that she would came in December, and she always told me that, always, always, always ... And I ... I was like, I believed her. I believed that she was going to come, but she never, never, never came. So, afterwards, when she told me she would come at such and such a time, or in a month, or in a year, I never believed her again. And then, I made myself believe that I was not going to live with her anymore. And then when I was living with my grandmother, I got used to it, and, and, and, because we were, I had my cousins there, and we played and everything, and so little by little, the hurt passed. And this is how I, I, I got used to this life without my mother. But I always missed her because...I mean, I was seven years old, and I got used to my mother being there with me, that is, that she would always be there with me ... And then, that she would leave .... I mean, she didn't tell me she was going to leave me.

Albeit unintentionally, caretakers often added to the children's confusion and distrust in others by lying to them about the parent's whereabouts, the expected date of return, or by keeping a deafening silence around the parents' immigration altogether.

Similar to Rita's account, for years Carla's family made her believe that her mother was working in a city nearby and would soon return.

I never knew that my mom had come here, never. Because I was 5 years old and my mother told me that she was going to work, and I knew that she worked in another town. And then time passed and I did not see her anymore. I did not see her again, and... and I asked my grandma, "Where is my mom?" And she said to me, "She is working". "But she did not come back", I said. But... and she would tell me, maybe to appease me, but I would say, "it is taking her too long". And so much time went by, so much time.... And my mom wasn't there, my mom, I didn't see her.... And then one day an uncle told me, "Your mom is in the United States", "What is it? What is the United States?", "It is a place far away", he said. And that is when I started to cry, because I didn't see her again. It was very difficult.

In the case of Isabela, the mother's absence and the father's death made the world so unsafe that even relatives should no longer be trusted.

And then, we left to my father's funeral, and all, and when we returned home, ah..., we had left the keys with an aunt, just in case. Because we didn't know if we were going to come back soon, or what. So, my cousins took the keys and took everything, all our clothes... they stole everything. They only left the furniture, but yes, they stole our clothes and all. And when we arrived with my aunt to pick things up, we saw that there was nothing there....

One of the functions of parents, particularly when their children are young, is that of translator of the outside world and of reality. It is as if, because children have not been around very long, it is up to the adults around them to help them interpret and make sense of reality. From this perspective, the combination of half-lies and poor communication contributed to these children feeling not only a sense of doubt in how they perceived the reality around them, but also that they could not count on adults to help them understand that reality. In some unfortunate cases, such as Isabela's, adults could not even be trusted as keepers of the children's belongings.

Fathers Will Be Boys

If mothers were overall seen as sacrificing and responsible, fathers, for the most part, sounded like unruly, irresponsible children themselves. With the exception of Isabela's father, who ended up dead, none of the others seemed ready for the task of parenthood. Suzana, Rita, and Carla saw their fathers disappear soon after the mother's departure, and all male participants mentioned their fathers' alcoholism. In Luis's case, the parents' separation was caused by the father's alcoholism, and Jorge's father lost a promising career as a soccer player because of his drinking. Alex's father was fired from a job in the U.S. that would have sponsored the children's immigration. Because of that, their trip was delayed for 5 or 6 years. And yet, all males tried to minimize or excuse the father's flaws. Alex laughed as he referred to the father's years of unemployment due to alcoholism as his "years of vacation" while the mother paid bills and ensured that the children were being cared for,

> in those 3 years that my dad took like, a vacation drinking [laughs], my mom was working and was carrying the whole bills. . . . The rent, and you know how expensive rent is here … and she sent money for us; and my mother was the only one who was working.

The girls interviewed, on the other hand, seemed less forgiving of their fathers' misconduct. Carla suggested that if it weren't for her father's irresponsibility, her mother probably would not have left to the U.S.,

> My father, I believe that … Well, they were young and I think they weren't serious, and they had two children already. And my mom was very disappointed with my father. I believe that if my father had been more responsible, or if he loved her, I believe that we, I think things would be different. Maybe we wouldn't be here, who knows?

Suzana could not contain her anger as she told me of how her father disappeared virtually immediately after the mother's departure.

> When I was a year old, like, they [my parents] were having problems in their job, and like, the company broke down. So she [my mother] had to quit, so you know? They got laid off; they had no choice. So she told my father, you know, "Leave with me", like, and he was like, "No, I've got to stay with the baby", you know? And that was all a lie because after my mom left, he moved out. And he never cared for me, like, he would come and visit me, like, once a year. And he lived like,

5 minutes, 15 minutes away from me. It was not like he lived
in the other side of the country, you know?

To this day, Suzana feels angry and mistrustful of her father.
Recently Suzana became an American citizen, which makes her
eligible to sponsor her father's application for immigration. To her, this
explains his recent efforts to renew contact with her.

> I found out lately, since everything is so hard in Colombia,
> that he has been looking for me, so that he can, he wants to see
> me, that he loves me, and that maybe he could come here...
> and I was like, "No". What does he think? That I am going to
> get residency for him? I would have to be crazy.... I would
> give to anybody else but him. He is the least [last?] person I
> would give it to. I am sorry, but that is the truth. I am sorry,
> but I cannot take that risk. Because, how? How? I mean,
> come on, you know? I tell my mom, "Put yourself in my
> shoes. I am his daughter!! I did not ask him to bring me into
> this world!" If I had told him, you have to bring me into this
> world, and you have to do this for me, I would understand,
> you know? "She made me do it." But I did not even know
> that I was going to come here! No, he has to look after his
> responsibility. I don't have no reason why I should lift a finger
> to help him come [emphatic] *when he didn't lift a finger to
> help me!*

The Emotional Price of Ignorance

Even for the children who interpreted the parents' immigration as self-
sacrificing, some of the parents' actions contributed to the children
feeling insecure and unsure that adults could be trusted. It seems that a
combination of ignorance and guilt influenced how the parents and
families approached the events around the parents' departure and
absence. Parents and grandparents lacked information and
understanding of how important it would be to include and explain to
the children what was happening in the family: the need for the parents
to immigrate, and their plans to leave the children in the care of

relatives. Maybe because they did not know how to relay that information in a developmentally appropriate manner, they told themselves that the children would not understand or would not tolerate the stress that such information would generate. Therefore, the adults justified to themselves the cruelty of their silence by telling themselves that the children would be better protected if kept out of the conversations altogether. It could also be that the parents were trying to protect themselves from their own sense of guilt and pressure over the need, maybe even the desire, to leave behind the problems, the past, poverty, and the children themselves.

SEPARATION AND EMOTIONAL DEVELOPMENT

Finally, by the end of this project, I hoped I would have a better understanding about the impact of separation in the participants' emotional development. Under what circumstances would they become more prone to develop internalizing symptoms of mental illness, such as depression and anxiety ? When were they more likely to externalize their distress and present symptoms of conduct disorders, drug use, and poor academic achievement? In my clinical experience working with children separated from their mothers or fathers, I found that there seemed to be a greater incidence of family conflict, involvement with gangs, affective disorders, and a pervasive lack of interest in school in families with a history of separation and piecemeal immigration. However, this was a skewed sample, considering that all such children had been identified as needing mental health services and treatment. Most of the participants in this project, however, had not been referred or received counseling or psychotherapy. Despite the very small number of participants, this hopefully represented a broader, less biased sample compared to the children I saw at the mental health center.

In this section I will present the participants' opinion on how they think this life experience affected them. In addition, the analysis of the sand trays seemed most appropriate to apply as I addressed the question of emotional development. Therefore, results of the sand tray analysis will be presented at the end of this section. Finally, the coding categories that seemed most relevant to offer some insight in the effect of separation in the children's emotional development are listed in Table 7.

Table 7. Coding categories:
Separation and Emotional Development

FREE NODES	TREE NODES		
	DAMAGED GOODS	HEROES	LOVE
Guilt	Culture as damaged	Culture as hero	Spoiled
War			
Shame	Life as damaged	Life as hero	
Losses			
Trauma	Self as damaged		

As mentioned earlier, with exception of Rita and Carla, all other participants did poorly in school. Rita, Carla, and Suzana presented as highly anxious, and in Carla's case, thinking was disorganized. Although data collection did not include a clinical evaluation for symptoms of psychopathology, there was a clear sense that Rita, Carla, Suzana, Jorge, and Isabela had developed symptoms of depression and anxiety in response to the numerous losses and trauma they endured.

When asked how they thought the prolonged separation had affected them, Isabela and Alex's answers gave me the feeling of a loss that would never be repaired. Isabela felt it was particularly difficult to go through adolescence without the support of her mother or father. When asked how he felt when he thought about the time he was separated from his parents, Alex said: "I don't feel anything.... Like... With my dad, we didn't play around with them, play football, and they didn't teach how to play Nintendo, soccer... That is all." Alex also seemed to feel he should only rely on himself to solve his problems. When asked whom he currently felt close to, Alex said,

Right now? Actually nobody now. I am so hard to express myself... If I have a problem I keep it on my mind... I ... I look for advice, but I don't talk about my problems... See, if something happens to me, why would I talk to other people? What are they going to do about it? They are not going to solve my problems... If I broke up with my girlfriend, and I go talk to my friend... what is he gonna do about it?

Nothing... and sometimes they get bored, you know? So, that is life... You were born lonely, by yourself, so you got to keep your problems to yourself too. You have to solve it by your own thinking and experience; you got to find your own solution.

In this touching segment, Alex seems to feel deeply isolated and concerned that he will bore other people, bringing further loss and abandonment. He seems to fear that seeking help would be interpreted as a sign of need and weakness, and there is always the risk of realizing that he is not worthy of help. Therefore, better not ask. Although in his statement, Alex sounds to be searching for independence and self-reliance, characteristics of the normal task of individuation during adolescence, there is an also an unquestionable sense of hopeless and sadness.

For Isabela, the loss of her mother, and later of her father, caused her to distance herself from other people and to doubt her own ability to feel love for others. "Oh, and also it was that, it was as if not having my mother made me... as if, I don't know, not to feel much love for other people." Isabela believed that because her mother was not there to teach her how to love others, she did not develop this skill and capacity appropriately. Another long-term effect of the separation was a pervasive sense of loss. Isabela seemed to struggle as she tried to explain to me what she saw as the consequence of the long separation from her mother.

Well, it continues being a good relationship, even though at times I think that something got lost. Something, because... it is not the same because ... Ok, when the mother is away, the person growths up, growths up, I mean... I mean... For example, my mother came here and rebuilt her life, and I had to stay there, and go on with my life. But it wasn't, my life was not the same because I missed her. And as I was growing up, it was like, it was hard for me because my mother wasn't there, and also because it was like, it was as if part of the love one feels for her mother gets lost. One always has the hope that she will see her mother, and all, but it is not the same as one sees her again... So it was as if I was a little afraid because I didn't know how she would react if I gave her a hug, or something. But little by little it went away.

Some participants saw many advantages in being raised in Latin America, and by their grandmothers. They were taught to be polite and respectful, highly valued traits in the Latino culture. For Luis, being raised by his grandmother also meant escaping the influence of gangs and violence, which resulted is a sense of mutual pride: *"I feel proud that she raised me because the children my age are, they go around with cigarettes, bad habits, bad choices, in gangs, and all that. Yes, well yes, she feels proud because I have no addictions."* Jorge also talked about feeling proud of his mother and in fact being able to trust her more as result of her sacrifice to come to the U.S. for her family.

Patterns of Sand Trays

The interpretation of sand trays is not always definitive due to its intuitive, non-operational quality. Therefore, the data analysis done through interpretation of sand trays is less conclusive when compared to data analysis done through coding. Despite this fact, I felt that it would be valuable to present some findings throughout the analysis of the sand trays, even if for the sole purpose of raising questions or facilitating the exploration of this method in future projects.

Sand trays were analyzed by looking at the formal aspects of the construction (such as the number of miniatures and categories used), the developmental level of the constructions, and the complexity and organization of the images represented. Then, the content of the constructions was analyzed. Content analysis included the approach of the sandplayer to the task, verbalizations during the task, title of the sand trays, and the stories provided to explain certain aspects of the construction. This approach to sand tray interpretation is known as the Erica Method of sand tray analysis (Sjolund & Schaefer, 1994). Please refer to Appendix C for a complete list of the elements considered and Appendix E for a sample of a sand tray analysis.

The participants' sand trays were then mapped using the Ryce-Menuhin (1992) suggested mapping approach. Figures 3 and 8 were the two figures I focused to help me understand the meaning behind those constructions. Appendix C lists the complete list of figures used in the mapping method of analysis, and Appendix E contains a sample of the interpretation of the sand tray for one of the participants.

Both sand trays built by Rita were empty and bare, characteristics often seen in sand trays of depressed patients. In fact, there was something disturbing about Rita' sand tray. Instead of placing the human figures standing up, using the sand on the box to provide support for those figures, as most people will do, Rita simply threw the figures on the sand, so that they all just lie on the ground. It seemed that Rita was trying to avoid relating to any of the figures that represented important persons in her life.

During the entire time Suzana was being interviewed, her speech was very rapid, a characteristic often seen in individuals with anxious or manic symptoms, and during the sand tray task Suzana had much difficulty containing her anxiety. She kept playing with the miniatures and talking to me incessantly, despite instruction to *build* a world. Playing with the sand tray instead of using it to build a scene is most commonly seen in seven, eight year-old children. In fact, all participants that presented as anxious spoke almost incessantly as they engaged in the task of building the sand tray.

Each of the seven participants built one sand tray at the end of each of the two interviews. As I spread the photographs of all 14 sand trays across the table, I noticed that one striking feature of virtually all fourteen sand trays was the inclusion of two houses in each of the trays. This could represent these children's feelings of actually having two homes and their ambivalence about being in the U.S. instead of in their country of origin. Carla reminisced about the days spent with her grandmother in their modest home, and Suzana became very emotional as she explained to me the meaning of each miniatures used in her first sand tray, in which she chose to picture her grandmother's city and country homes.

Suzana spoke enthusiastically about how happy she felt the weekends spent with her grandma in the country house. Then, her affect changed as she realized how much she missed those days, and expressed regret for having to immigrate to the U.S. Suzana talked about how disappointed she still feels about her life in the U.S. and how resentful she feels about the way her mother treats her. She then titled that first tray, "What I Gave Up to Be Here". Suzana was not an isolated case in the way she depicted the world in her country of origin.

Although my instructions were purposely very general and vague (to "build a world using the miniatures on the shelf"), many of the participants used the opportunity to build a scene that represented their home back in South and Central America. That occurred especially after the first interview, where the focus was on these children's lives and recollection about the period of separation from their parents.

Another feature of many of the trays was the desire to help the parents or the caretakers. Alex built a scene were he would give his parents a restaurant and a farm, and in fact titled the tray, "The Future of my Parents", whereas Luis "built" a house surrounded by a pretty garden and placed a figure representing his grandmother at the front entrance.

There was a striking difference between the sand trays built after the first interview compared to the ones built after the second meeting. Whereas the first trays seemed more uplifting and cheerful, there was a sense of sadness and deprivation in the scenes of the second trays. As the reader might remember, the focus of the first interview was the time the participants spent with their caretakers in the country of origin, whereas the second interview focused on the participants' memories about moving to the U.S. and reuniting with the parents. The first trays done by all participants had a larger number of miniatures and categories (i.e., plants, minerals, animals, human figures, etc.) compared to their second trays. Except Alex and Carla, all other participants used on average 10 more miniatures in their first trays compared to their second trays. According to the Erica method for analyzing sand trays, using several miniatures and choosing a wide range of categories are more typical of emotionally healthy and mature individuals. Fewer pieces and restricted categories, on the other hand, can be interpreted as a sign of arrest in emotional development or emotional difficulties. Could this indicate that the participants were emotionally healthier while in their country of origin, and less motivated or even depressed after moving to the U.S.?

By convention, the bottom of sand trays is always painted blue, so that the builder can depict bodies of water by removing the sand from particular areas in the tray. Clinicians who use art in their work often think of water as a symbol for nurturance and warmth. Interestingly, 5 out of the 7 participants chose to illustrate lakes, ponds, rivers, or the ocean in their first trays. For the group of trays built following the second interview, however, only 2 out of the 5 participants included the "picture" of a lake in their sand trays. One could speculate that whereas these children felt emotionally fulfilled as they remembered their days with the caretakers, the world with their parents in the U.S. was dry and emotionally bare.

I chose to concentrate on maps 3 and 8 of the Ryce-Menuhin approach to sand tray analysis (please refer to Appendix C for more information on mapping and Appendix B for details on the pictures of all sand trays photographed) . Of note was the fact that the participants that reported less distress regarding their life history and relationship with caretakers or parents used a range of miniatures in the part of the tray usually thought of as representing the "self" (see Appendix C, figure 8 of the Ryce-Menuhin assessment). Those who presented with more disturbed affect or reported more difficulty in adjustment and conflict with their parents often had a very empty presentation of "self" in their trays. Furthermore, there was a marked difference in patterns of the trays using map 8 as reference. Whereas for the group of sand trays done after the first interview the location designated as "self" was more full and alive, the same "mapping location" in the group of sand trays done following the second interview was more empty, with less "going on".

Map 3 of the Ryce-Menuhin Mapping approach divides the sand tray horizontally in half. Whereas the upper half is often interpreted as representing more deliberate, conscious processes of the sandplayer, the bottom half seems to illustrate and be associated with internal conflicts and emotional aspects of the self that are less deliberate, less available to the awareness of the sandplayer. Looking at the 14 photos of sand trays in Appendix B, one cannot help but notice how many of the trays in fact have such distinction clearly divided. In fact, 6 out of the 14 trays had fences, rivers, lines of cars and trucks divide the tray artificially into upper and bottom halves. The remaining trays, although lacking these concrete boundaries, had a marked difference in "feel" between the two halves. For some, the scene illustrated in the upper half contrasted with a completely empty bottom half, for example.

Despite the small sample and other limitations of this project, some of the findings observed in previous research using sand trays as an instrument to differentiate among populations were also found in this study. Among the participants that presented as significantly anxious or as having trouble adapting to their new family and environment, a lesser imaginative use of the miniatures was observed. Number of miniatures used, range of categories that participants chose, as well as approach to the task was also significantly distinct among participants, with the more troubled participants using fewer number and categories of miniatures. Finally, it seems that among males, who in general had more trouble with verbal expression, an increased effort was observed in their approach to the task of the sand tray construction. They were surprisingly creative and resourceful in the final product and seemed more pleased and at ease with the activity compared to the females. All participants used the opportunity to share with me their recollection regarding their life in the native country, and almost all chose to include the caretaker in the first sand tray.

SUMMARY

Contextual factors, cultural norms, and expectations seemed to greatly influence how children internalized and adapted to the departure and prolonged separation from their parents. The family's need for survival, and the parents' dependability in maintaining contact and in continuously providing for the material needs of the family (even if from a distance), seemed to improve the outcome of these children's adjustment. Another key element in these children's adaptation to their parents' absence was the message that caretakers gave these children during the period of separation. During childhood, most of us encounter perceived or real threats to our existence. Because as children we lack the capacity for self-reflection, we need adults to provide holding and reflecting for us. For the children interviewed for this project, the caretakers' reflections and interpretations around the parents' departure and absence became these children's most important source of explanation of their external reality. The caretakers' interpretation of the parents' reason for immigration was, therefore, internalized by these children without much questioning or revision. However, even with the most benign set of external circumstances, many of these children could not help but feel unloved and rejected at times. Such duality of emotions and cognition seemed to be part of a larger, overarching theme of duality that permeated this project: separation versus reunification; sacrifice versus abandonment; the felt-obligation of loyalty to caretakers versus the expected sense of loyalty towards parents, the desire to remain in the country of origin versus the need to join the parents in the U.S.; feeling rejected versus feeling special . . . the list seems to go on forever. Whereas caretakers played a key role during the period of separation, parents' behaviors and attitudes, overt and covert messages became essential in how the children adjusted to the reunification with their parents upon arrival in the U.S.. In Chapter 6 I will explore the key elements that influenced the process of reunification among these children and families.

The Process of Reunification

Alex: "It was kind of hard to get along with our parents because we didn't understand each other for... we did not know each other for 13 years, so it was hard to understand."

Almost intrinsic to the nature of the qualitative method for research, unexpected themes and questions begging for answers often emerge in the process of data analysis and interpretation. To no surprise, as I reviewed and organized the data, I found that another aspect of the separation had to also be addressed: the reunification with the parents and adjustment to life in the U.S. As I studied the data and the interview segments, I found that the children's memories about the period of reunification with the parents were also important to understand their current functioning and attachment patterns. Without creating a whole new project within the original proposed study, I felt the need to address this other aspect of separation. Therefore, as I approached this new theme, I tried to keep it limited to aspects of the reunification with the parents that were relevant to better understand the impact of separation from them. Therefore, Chapter 6 is less extensive than the previous chapter, and its organization does not mirror that of Chapter 5.

In this chapter I present findings that may help us better understand the participants' memories and thoughts about the period of reunification with their parents and these children's views on how their current relationship to their parents evolved. What events during reunification reinforced the children's belief that the parents' immigration was driven by the desire to help their families? What aspects of that experience hindered the children's view of the parents as altruistic? How did the children's immigration to the U.S. impact their internal working models of self and others? Finally, I tried to explore which factors and events may have enhanced or impaired the children's psychological health and emotional development as they tried to adjust to their family and to life in the U.S. By answering these questions, I hoped to get some insight into which elements in the process of reunification were beneficial and which ones were detrimental to the well-functioning of these children and families. Once these elements were identified, a list of appropriate interventions could then be suggested to professionals and practitioners working with this population.

ABANDONMENT OR SACRIFICE?

Some events during the first years of reunification with the parents seemed to confirm previously held beliefs these children had about the parents' motives to leave them as a sacrifice they made for the children's sake. Other events and parental behaviors created even further conflict and emotional distress for these children.

The Children's Turn

For many of the children interviewed for this project, there was the explicit message that, in the same way that the parents sacrificed for the well-being of the children, now that they were in the U.S., it was their turn to make sacrifices for their family. It was their turn to pay the parents back for the hardships they endured to bring the kids to the U.S. Carla, for example, remembers how her mother placed on her the responsibility to compensate for all the sacrifices she made for the daughter.

> And my mother would say to me, 'No, you have to go on.... If you go back... it can't be, 'cause you were away from me for 9 years... it can't be'. And then I thought, and I said to myself,

'Well, my mother made many sacrifices, and it took her over 9
years to bring my brother and I legally. And it was very hard, I
imagine'. And when I arrived, I found the environment very
disappointing. But, well, I went on...

In Alex's case, despite the impression of the father giving his
children the choice to stay or to return to Guatemala, on a more careful
interpretation, this choice seems illusory. In this segment, Alex in fact
seemed to feel great pressure to meet the father's expectations and
needs. His sense of loyalty and obligation to his family is clear.

After that year that we were here, then we got our green card,
all us three. After we got our green card, then we wanted to go
back to Guatemala. But we .... it would have been hard to... I
told my dad, 'Do you want me to stay in Guatemala or here?'
'I prefer to...' he'd say, 'I want you to stay here because we
are your family and if you need something or if you want us to
talk ... we wasted a lot of time. We didn't have you when you
were children, little, so we want to have you when you are
adults, you know?' So I told him we would stay here.

Although the perspective of the parents was not part of this project,
their grief and needs can often be heard in the voices of the children.
Like Carla's mother, Alex's father also seemed to feel the need to
compensate for the years of absence and the lost opportunity to see his
children grow up. So, once again, these children were placed in the
position to protect their parents' emotional well-being by making a
sacrifice and staying in the U.S. so that their parents would be given the
opportunity to enjoy their sons and daughters' company.

Some participants seemed to experience many of the ideal
conditions that made the separation and reunification the least
damaging to family functioning and the least negative to their self-
concept as possible. Some of those conditions included continued
contact with the absent parent, open communication among family
members, a kind and consistent caretaker during the separation, and
parents who were married and living together. However, even these
children found it extremely difficult to express to their mother how they
really felt about being in the U.S. In this passage, for example, Isabela

trades places with her mother, assuming the role of parent by trying to solve the mother's problems and protect her mother from sadness.

> We almost didn't talk [my mother and I] ... Well, she, yes, she would ask me how I felt and all, but I sometimes, I, so that she wouldn't feel bad, I would tell her, "I am fine"... But in reality, I was not fine. But I knew that if we went back to my country, she wouldn't know ... I mean, my mom wouldn't know how to survive, because everything is very difficult there, and it is hard to find a job and all. And I didn't want my mother to feel bad. So I would tell her that I was fine, but that was not true.

Same House, But No Time

Children resented the long hours parents spent at work, especially when they first arrived in the U.S. Despite the fact that they now lived in the same house, the parents again recreated the feeling of abandonment because of the amount of time they spent away from their children. For Suzana, the mother's unavailability created much resentment and made it difficulty for their relationship to develop.

> And now she tells me, 'Now when I have time you don't want to talk to me... It is not fair...'. 'When I wanted to talk to you, you don't have time... so now...' I know two wrongs don't make one right, but what makes one wrong thing is that before she had no time to ... for me, what makes her think that now I have time for her? You know, I know it is not right, but that is how I feel... 'You don't have time for me, why am I gonna have time for you', you know?

As Alex talked about how he would prefer to live in Guatemala, if given the choice, I got the sense that he was in fact talking about how he resented the parent's absence due to work. Alex seemed to be actually talking about the fact that his parents never have time for him or his sisters, "you see, in this country work kills you a lot, because you got to work, work, work... too much. Even you don't know what day it is because of the work...." This feeling was confirmed when Alex talked about his sand tray, later in the interview. He again brought up the topic of hard work, but now associated to the fact that his parents worked so hard in this country that they never had time, and his desire to give them a farm in Guatemala so that they can have a good life.

Some of these children felt the need to express their pain through anger and rejection of the parent. The parents, however, were ill prepared to contain the child's negative feelings towards them and, for the most part, handled the situation quite poorly. In their fear of being rejected by their children, they seemed to either distance themselves emotionally from the children or attempt to use their power and authority to shape a loving relationship.

The Wish to Rewrite the History of Abandonment

Most of the participants mentioned that they did not expect to be the ones to come to join the parents and live in the U.S. As Luis said, "I knew that she was going to come to this country, but that she would soon come back home, to live with us ... like, normal".

Isabela, Carla, and Rita also had no idea that they would be the ones expected to join their mother in the U.S. Isabela stated repeatedly how she hoped that her mother would be the one to return. It is also interesting to see how she, for the first and only time, mentions in this segment her doubts about her mother's love for her and her siblings.

I remember that we always wished that she returned... Well, my brothers always wrote to her asking her to return, to return. But I knew that she couldn't go back. And yes, I did want to be with her, and I knew that I would see her again, but I never thought that it would be here, in this country. Because I never thought I would come here. I think that none of my brothers imagined we would come here. We thought that maybe we would move somewhere else, and that my mom would come, and because there were no more problems, there was no war .... We thought it would be different, but .... And then, when my mother got her residency, and all that... and for us too... and that is why we came here... But I wanted that she return... but she couldn't... I don't know... I used to think that she did not want to go back, and when I was little, I used to think that maybe she did not want to return, that maybe she preferred to be in this country instead of our country .... I used to think many things... that maybe she forgot about us, that she did not want us anymore... like that.

These children hoped and expected the parents to be the ones to return. As I read through the transcripts, it seemed that such desire stood for some other need: a metaphor for their need to see themselves as the ones who leave the parent behind. The participants were now entering adolescence and preparing for their developmental task of "second individuation" (Blos, 1967). It occurred to me that then maybe these children were unconsciously trying to create a scenario where the parents come back and were now available to "be left. Now Anna Freud's quote seemed gain a whole new dimension. If for Ms. Freud, *"The mother's job is to be there to be left"*, for the children left behind, *The mother's job is to return, so that she can be there to be left.*

REUNIFICATION AND IMPACT ON INTERNAL WORKING MODEL OF SELF AND OTHERS

When studying the children's memories of the time they were separated from the parents (Chapter 5), it seemed more appropriate to treat the concepts of representational models of self and others as two separate sets of data. However, as I tried to take the same approach when analyzing the segments where the participants talk about the period of reunification to the parents, such strategy did not prove effective. It seemed that these two concepts were so connected and interdependent in these children's processing of the experience, that breaking up the segments would have made the analysis less effective. Therefore, the findings related to these two concepts will be presented simultaneously.

Expectations, Criticisms and Disappointment

As we saw in chapter 5, the children often equated being loved with being spoiled. Therefore, if in anger, parents told them that they were spoiled, the children internalized those statements as proof that they did not deserve to be loved or cared for. Many participants talked about feeling immensely hurt by the parents' criticisms and their comments that the children had been spoiled by the caretakers. Parents seemed to often disappoint the children's dreams and expectations of how the relationship would unfold. This resulted in the children often feeling emotionally abandoned by the parents, although they were physically reunited. As I read the segments where children described their relationship to the parents when they were first reunited, there is a pervasive sense of frustration. In addition, there is the sense of a gross mismatch between these children's fantasies and expectations and the reality they come in contact with upon arrival.

In addition to being criticized and let down, Suzana felt that the mother would not protect her against the criticism of family friends. In fact, according to Suzana, her mother often encouraged these friends to be disrespectful or abusive towards Suzana.

> She [my mother] would tell her friends, " Oh, Suzana is so rude, Suzana is so bad, she is this, she is that" and everybody would be like, screaming at me, telling me "why are you doing that to your mom?" So that made me hate... kind of hate her more, you know? ... Like, you know, "you are not the mother that I expected it to be", you know? Because I always wanted for me to be with my mom, like cool, you know?... like my cousins used to be. And I looked at her and I was like, "you are not the person I was expecting it to be".

From the discourse of the participants, one gets the impression that they felt the disappointment was mutual. Parents, children, and life as a whole did not seem to match anybody's dreams and expectations about what would happen once the family was reunited. In an almost identical echo of Suzana's complaints, Carla also expressed deep disappointment for how her real mother turned out to be, compared to her fantasies and expectations.

> Uh.... Let's see, from 1986 to 1996, about ten years of separation, and ... and I got to know her more, and she is ... she is serious in a lot of ways, she is serious about it. She had me so strict, and that is when we used to argue almost all the time, and argue, argue, and argue, and I was like, 'No, I want to go back because this can't be my mother'. And then I

always used to say, 'I grew so much for years... I used to, I
felt at times so alone, and wanted my mommy to be here, and
now you don't want to behave like you are supposed to
behave?'

In another segment, it is clear how her mother also seems
disappointed of how the daughter is and behaves. Carla's mother
blames herself and the separation for Carla's personality, and such
criticism leaves a deep mark on Carla's concept of herself.

And she [my mother] said to me, 'if you had been with me
you would not think like this. You are too serious, too angry.
You raise your voice to me, you are like this, you are like
that...' And this was something that stayed with me.

Rita's disappointment and mistrust of her mother was increased by
the mother's attempts to destroy Rita's relationship with her caretakers.
Rita talked about how the mother failed to give Rita letters and photos
that her aunt and uncle had sent to her. Rita found those things by
accident and felt much anger towards the mother. Although afraid of
the mother's reaction, Rita decided to confront her.

So I didn't want to ask her because I knew she was going to
make a big scene, that we would fight and all that... but one
day – because I always thought 'why didn't she show them
[the pictures and letters] to me, why?' And then we were in
the car, and she told me that, yes, that she had showed them to
me.... That she showed them knowing that she had not... I
mean, she knew that what she did was wrong, and so she
lied.... I don't know why she does that....

The experience of reunification seemed to place the children's
internal working model of self and others under revision. Their
representational models were now being reshaped by the experiences
with the parents during the first years of reunification. Being criticized
by the parents often proved to be a new source of stress and injury in
these children's fragile sense of self and ability to trust in their parents.

This pattern seemed to again reinforce the children's belief that they did not deserve to be loved unconditionally.

School, Competency, Learning English

Staying in the U.S., making the relationship work, and being successful in school were common goals stated by the children interviewed. However, some participants felt that one of the parents' mistakes was to wait too long before bringing them to the U.S. They felt that it was much harder to learn the language, to adapt to a new society, and rebuild a relationship with the parents because they were older. Feeling socially and academically incompetent had a disastrous effect in their sense of self.

> We [Martha and I] are supposed to be a senior. But because they put us one year behind... we were supposed to graduate this year but we didn't have enough credits for English... So...That kind of makes me feel mad at my parents, you know? Because they should have bring us when we were little, so that we would know the system. Because now that we are older, it is hard to graduate from high school... it is not that hard because we understand the system, but it would have been better if ... it would save some time for us to learn the language, you know? Now my friends are going to university and I am still in high school ... I get kind of mad...

Suzana, Rita, and Carla also felt very insecure and incompetent as they tried to continue their education using a language completely unfamiliar. Carla talked at great length about the challenges she faced trying to adapt to the American school system, but she also mentioned how important some of her teachers had been during her first year living in the U.S.. These teachers greatly facilitated her process of adjusting to a new culture and way of life, often providing the support Carla lacked at home.

REUNIFICATION AND EMOTIONAL DEVELOPMENT

Finally, the process of adaptation to the American culture and to a new educational system, as well as the exposure to a different value system, in some cases helped the emotional development of some participants and, in other cases, contributed to their psychological distress. Many children felt the increased stress of adapting to their families, to a new social status and "pecking order" with a marked decrease in their support system. They no longer enjoyed the company of old friends and the sense of competency and ease that comes from being in one's own culture and environment. The underlying theme was of losses: losses that never seemed to end. There is strong evidence that experiencing too many losses during our formative years places us at increased risk to develop psychological problems and psychopathology (Bowlby, 1988; Harris & Bifulco, 1991). Whereas in chapter 5 I focused on the losses due to separation from the parents, here I look at the losses that reunification with the parents and immigration to the U.S. continued to bring to the lives of these children.

The Losses That Never Seem to End

Joining the parents in the U.S. was a journey full of hopes and expectations. For many of these children, it seemed to be their opportunity to make up for the losses they suffered in the past. However, as they arrived and watched the relationship fall short of their dreams, they once again were faced with further deprivation. Besides, many of the participants felt that the relationship with their parents would never recover from the lost time and lost connection.

As Alex talked about the first weeks after his arrival in the U.S., it became clear that unspoken grief, anger, poor communication, and lack of experience in dealing with each other made the process of reunification an enormous task and challenge for his family. And no matter which way he turned, there was a sense of another loss being just around the corner, ready to reveal itself.

> I was feeling sad because of my cousins, you know? We were like brothers, we separated, you know... it was _ of everybody there, _ of everybody here... So we were like, those couple weeks, everyday we were crying because we were not used to this system, and the language, and we didn't know our parents... and we were really sad because of them. We were,

like, I tell you, us 6, everybody had one person to talk about their problems, you know? Or to play with them... I remember with my cousin, we were always together. If he went to the store, I went with him; if I went to the park, he'd come with me ... and if we had problems with my other cousin, he would help me out to beat him up [laughs]. And you know, my sister, she helped her cousin to beat us up, you know? . . . So we were like that. So we were crying because of them and [because of] my aunt, because she helped my grandma to raise us .... And at first we would be sad, we didn't understand our parents, the way they wanted us to be. ... and the language ... It was hard. Those three problems we had...and then after that, my grandma was over here and she kind of dropped us off, and then she stayed for 2 or 3 months. I remember that. It was kind of hard, because for 3 months she was here and she helped us a lot. And after she left, then all the problems come, altogether.... Our parents, you know? ... We didn't have our grandma no more, our cousins, and we didn't have like... usually we wanted to talk to our family in Guatemala and our mom doesn't like us to use the phone too much. So, it was kind of those problems, you know? It was hard because we didn't get along together - we didn't understand each other, so ... But now, the time makes you learn...

In a very emotional tone, Rita talked about what she felt was the consequence of the separation in her relationship with her mother;

I used to think that, that maybe it was because I had just arrived, and all. But then I started to analyze it, and realized that ... that nothing would be like when I was little. Nothing will be the same ... and that is reality. And I believe that it is a reality I must accept, because I don't feel the same as to when I was little. Yes, I love her [my mother], because yes, I like her. But not as when I was little... I don't know... Because I would say, 'maybe it is because I just arrived, and so many things'... But it has been over two years, and nothing... Everything is stilling the same.

In addition to falling behind in school and having more difficulty learning a second language, not keeping pace with schoolmates represented for Alex another loss in an endless string of losses.

> Yeah, all my friends are graduating, so... Now my friend, the Bolivian dude, we are really close. When I came, he was here 2 years, 3 years when I came. So he knew the system here, and he usually take me out of the home. Because I didn't go out with nobody; I knew nobody... So he usually called me and we go play some soccer. So now he is graduating and I should be graduating with him and my other friends... So it really hurt me... but it is ok... I know I am gonna finish, so... it is one more year... Yeah, because they are taking the pictures for the seniors' book, and I would like to take those pictures with them, you know? But it is still good.

In one of his unusually emotional moments, Alex's voice trembled as he told me he would not be taking pictures with his Bolivian "dude". As I heard the stories told by Alex, Isabela, Suzana, and Rita, I realized that, in their short lives, these children had experienced so many losses that their tolerance to endure future losses was greatly reduced. Any event interpreted by them as being once again left behind was enough to open a gate of grief and sadness for which they had little internal resources to contain.

Parents and children lacked a common history, common memories and traditions. For Isabela and her mother, there was the awkwardness and the inability to re-engage once the family reunited. If on one hand, Isabela felt awkward in trying to approach the mother or give her a hug, her mother also did not know how to become part of her children's lives.

> And it was different because... I don't know, maybe she felt.... I feel that both of us were afraid. And because, the three of us came together, my brothers and I, and I remember that the three of us would lock ourselves in the bedroom and would remember things we went through, and all. We would laugh of things... of mischief we did, those things... And

sometimes my mother would stop by the door and listen to us, and it was as if she was also afraid ... Other times we were talking at the table and my mother did not know what we were talking about... or sometimes, she was talking and we didn't know..."

On a more hopeful note, many children talked about the advantages of being raised by their grandparents or in a Latin country. They believed that this gave them a better chance to learn to be polite and respectful, traits that are highly regarded in the Latino culture. But at the same time, one can clearly hear these children question the parents' ability to be competent as parents. Suzana spoke of how in Colombia children are taught to respect their elders and to talk appropriately, and as we saw in chapter 5, Luis felt proud to be raised by his grandmother, which he believes, sheltered him from a life of crime and addiction. In the segment below, Alex compares himself to his cousins who were raised by their own parents in the U.S.

> *Alex*: For example my cousin, my little cousins... doesn't respect their parents, his mom, he doesn't respect. So I would be like him, you know? [If I was raised here, by my parents] ...Because my grandma, she wanted us to show some respect to older persons, so I think my grandma gave us advice, and she showed us a lot of stuff for life, and how to respect other persons...
> *Author*: So you think that if you were always with your mother you wouldn't be as polite and respectful? ...knowing what to do?
> *Alex:* Maybe yes, maybe no. There would be a question mark because you know how the parents here always work.

Becoming an Adult

Maybe one way these children found to reconnect to their parents was when they started to relate to them as adults or equals. Isabela, for example, reported that once she became a mother herself, the relationship with her own mother improved, and she no longer acted out her resentment or anger. Alex seemed proud as he talked about taking his father out for dinner.

Yeah... now we work together, you see? When we go out,
like sometimes, me and my dad we usually go out Monday.
He usually invites me to go to any place I want to eat.... Then
we talk about stuff, you know? How is school, how are you
doing with your girls... how you are doing at the job, you
know? When I got money, I do the same thing with my dad.
So, if my dad is sleeping, I go and wake him up and say, "Did
you eat already?" And I will buy anything you want, and we
go and talk... Now we get along...

EFFECTS OF BEING INTERVIEWED

At the beginning of the second interview, I asked the participants how
they felt after our first interview, and whether they had any thoughts or
feelings triggered by their recollections and recount of their experience
that they wish to discuss. Some talked about giving it some thought or
wanting to correct some previous statement. Alex, for example, seemed
bothered by his lack of recall about the time his grandmother's house
caught on fire. In fact, he talked to his sister about the event, trying to
put the pieces together, and wanted to make sure he could correct some
of the details he gave me during the first meeting. Isabela talked to her
mother about the interview, and so did Jorge. In both cases, the parents
seemed curious and somewhat concerned about how they were being
portrayed by the children or perceived by me.

At the end of the interviews, I asked the adolescents participating
in this project about the effect and impact (if any) that telling me their
story had on their feelings and perceptions about the life events
discussed. Interestingly, the participants who used the interview as a
cathartic process seemed more enthusiastic when telling me how
beneficial they had found the experience to be. Those who had a more
reserved attitude were more evasive about elaborating on whether this
was a helpful process or not. In general, however, most of these
youngsters reported relief in being able, for the first time in many
cases, to talk to an adult without the fear of being criticized or judged
about their feelings and loyalties.

Luis was very guarded and seemed determined to portray his mother as flawless, the experience of separation as harmless, almost positive, and his life as very fulfilling. He seemed very invested in presenting a romantic, idyllic picture of his life. When asked about how he felt, Luis told me to become quite sad after our first interview. It occurred to me that maybe this process was a parallel process of his emotional experience with his mother. Because he felt he could not trust me to contain his negative feelings (by talking openly about them), he then had to go home and deal with his hurt and anger all on his own. Very much like a mirror of his relationship with his mother, he showed me a brave face to protect his mother and his image of the experience of separation, only to then be confronted with his real feelings all by himself. Further investigation about the validity of this process could be important for those of us working with individuals that had with similar life experiences.

SUMMARY

The process of adaptation to a new culture and new family seemed to take a toll even among the most well-adjusted participants in this study. The loss of contact with the surrogate parent, the loss of the feeling of optimum functioning in a familiar environment and culture, and the stress over losing the feeling of competency and mastery - so important during the years of adolescence – all had a negative impact on most of the participants. The children interviewed seemed to empathize with their parents' distress over the added responsibility to care for the newly arrived children, as these parents struggled to fulfill their roles as providers and parents. However, the participants felt again lonely and rejected as they were faced with long hours of loneliness and separateness in their new environments. In addition, these children often reported that their parents related to them in critical and demeaning ways, further undermining their sense of trust in their own self worth and their trust in important people in their lives. Finally, participants seemed to again feel compelled to take on the role of emotional guardians of their parents by colluding with the parents' decision to keep a vow of silence and secrecy around any feelings regarding the challenges faced by these families regarding their history of separation and reunification.

CHAPTER 7

Summary, Implications, Conclusions, Recommendations For Future Research.

This final chapter is divided into five sections. First, a brief summary of the purpose and design of this project is presented. Following is a summary of the findings brought to light through the analysis and interpretation of the data collected. Third, implications for practitioners working with this population in clinical settings are discussed. Next, a list of recommendations for future research on this topic is presented. Finally, general conclusions reached through this study are reported.

SUMMARY

Several events influenced how children separated in childhood interpreted and internalized the separation from the parents. The context leading to the parent's immigration; cohesiveness of opinions around the parent's motives and intentions within family members; the quality of the relationship with the parents before and after the separation; and the quality of care during the period of separation, all seemed important elements that contributed to the effect this event would have on these children's sense of self and others.

151

Purpose

The purpose of this study was to explore, describe, and better understand the experiences, perceptions, and memories of Latino adolescents and young adults reunited with their biological parents after prolonged separation during childhood because of piecemeal immigration patterns. The main hypothesis was that there was a core conflict in how children separated from their parents made sense of the parent's decision to leave, as they struggled between seeing the event as abandonment or as a sacrifice the parents made for the family. These two views were mediated by individual, family and cultural characteristics and influenced these children's internal working models. In turn, their representational models of self and others may have predisposed them to distinctive affective, cognitive, and behavioral patterns, and to difficulties in their close relationships.

Conceptual Framework

Attachment styles, individuation in adolescence, and cultural norms were the three main concepts used to approach this project. Attachment theory provided a useful framework to understand how childhood experiences shape who we become, and to how we relate to others and to the world around us. According to that theoretical approach, the specific ways one relates to self and others throughout life has its roots in the quality and characteristics of the relationship to the main caretaker in childhood. Furthermore, such patterns of attachment are also influenced by how people perceive, interpret, and integrate the memories of that relationship (Ainsworth, 1984, Ainsworth, 1991; Colin 1996b). Finally, disruption in the relationship with the main attachment figure seems to place individuals at risk for emotional and relational difficulties in adulthood (Adam, 1982; 1994; Bates & Bayles, 1988; Brennan & Shaver, 1995; Brown, 1982; Harris & Bifulco, 1991; Hazan & Shaver, 1987/ 1990; Kobak & Hazan, 1991; Shaver & Brennan, 1992). Based on these premises, the perception and memories of the participants around their relationships to their parents and caretakers would greatly influence their representational models of self and others, and how they would relate to others and to their environment.

Adolescence is one of the developmental stages when the attachment system is being revised. During those years, individuals try to resolve issues of separation and individuation from the parents and family of origin and start establishing emotional connections to potential partners (Blos, 1967; Kroeger, 1996). Adolescence is also the stage of human development when one strives to establish an autonomous identity. Autonomy is defined as the acquisition of self-governance, i.e., a set of behaviors that reflects increased self-regulation (Hill & Holmbeck, 1986). Other authors define autonomy and self-regulation not only in terms of expressed behaviors and attitudes, but also in terms of transferring responsibility and decision making to the adolescent (Collins & Luebker, 1991; Holmbeck, 1992). Positive feelings about one's own sense of competency, such as pride, esteem, and confidence in the ability to achieve goals and to handle stress (Blatt & Blass, 1990) are also related to autonomy. Taking those theories into consideration, I anticipated that, due to the special circumstances that being recently reunited with parents represented for the participants of this study, the process of individuation from their parents might take on distinctive features for the adolescents interviewed. It could be that the dynamics in these families was to try to re-engage the adolescents rather than support them in their effort to reach to the outside world (or practice their developing autonomy) as part of their main developmental task. Therefore, taking in consideration the importance of the developmental tasks during adolescence seemed an essential lens to use in approaching this project. Finally, I predicted that another important factor to consider in the study of this group was their specific cultural norms and expectations regarding family relations, attachment styles, and adolescent development. These norms would very likely influence the process of individuation among these children considering that actions seen in one culture as normative can be interpreted as abnormal and unhealthy under the lens of another culture (Arcia & Johnson, 1998; Freeberg & Stein, 1996). Based on these assumptions, this project was designed and conducted using these three main conceptual frameworks: Attachment theory, process of individuation in adolescence, and cultural norms of family relations and adolescent development among Latinos.

Research Questions

In this project I tried to obtain a first-hand account of how adolescents
and young adults who were separated from their parents during their
childhood later conceptualize and integrate that experience. My main
hypothesis was that children separated from their parents struggle
between seeing the parent's absence as abandonment and, at times, as a
sacrifice the parents made for the family and the children's welfare.
The way they interpret the parents' behaviors shape their internal
working models of self and others. That, in turn, may predispose those
individuals to secure or insecure patterns of affect, cognition, behavior,
and particular relational styles. Finally, it may increase their risk to
develop emotional problems.

The specific questions I intended to answer through this project
were:

1. What meaning did young Central American immigrants separated
    from their parents in childhood gave to that experience? How did
    they explain to themselves the parent's decision to immigrate and
    leave them behind? Was there a conflict between how they
    integrated the experience at the cognitive versus at the emotional
    level? Was there a common meaning given by the participants to
    the experience of being left and to the decision made by the
    parent? If so, what were some of the commonly shared cultural,
    community, familial, and individual characteristics?

2. What was the impact of separation on these participants'
    representational or internal working models of self? If there was
    indeed a dichotomy between conceptualizing the separation as
    abandonment versus *sacrifice*, what role did it play in the
    participants' internal working model of self?

3. What was the impact of separation on these participants'
    representational or internal working models of others? If there was
    indeed a dichotomy between conceptualizing the separation as
    abandonment versus *sacrifice*, what role did it play in the

participants' internal working model of others and in their current relationship with their parents?

4.   How did this life experience affect the emotional development of the participants? What role, if any, did that experience and its interpretation play in the participants' risk to develop psychological problems?

Subjects

Four females and three males from Central and South America, ages 15 to 19 were identified and interviewed. They arrived from Central and South America within the past 2 to 7 years after being separated from their mothers and/or fathers for at least 5 years, with onset of separation between birth and age nine.

Methods and Procedures

This study followed a topical design, focusing on the issue of separation from parents and the ways it affected the relationship with self and others. The approach was collaborative, with the participants taking the role of experts. Two individual, semi-structured interviews where conducted with each participant. They were audiotaped and lasted about 90 minutes each. The interviews were transcribed in their entirety. Participants were asked to "build a scene" by placing miniatures on a wooden box filled with sand (sand tray) at the end of each interview, and the sand trays were photographed. The first interview focused on the participants' recollections about the period of separation. The second interview focused mainly on the process of immigration to the U.S., these children's memories of those first months, current relationship with their parents and significant others, adjustment to American schools, and their goals for the future. Standard ethical guidelines in research and clinical practice were followed to protect the participants and their families, and a small stipend was available to the participants.

Data Analysis

Coding was the main method of analysis used to support the discussion and conclusions. Certain segments of the interviews were identified and coded because they formed important patterns of response across participants, leading to the creation of coding categories. The N-Vivo Nud*ist computer software (1999) was used to create codes and categories, identify relevant segments, organize memos, and for other data management tasks. A total of 30 coding categories (or nodes) were identified and created. I also looked for metaphors to understand individual and collective meaning of the participants' experiences.

Two different approaches to sand tray analyzes were used as complimentary methods of interpretation: The sand trays were mapped following the Ryce-Menuhin method for mapping sand trays (1992), and they were then classified using the most relevant elements as proposed by the Erica Method of Assessment (Sjolund & Schaefer, 1994). Using these guidelines helped me bring to light other relevant issues and raised questions for further investigation. Finally, the segments in Spanish that were used in the final text were translated and back-translated for accuracy. Quotes in Spanish and the English translation became part of the body of the text so that the voices of all participants could be preserved in their integrity.

FINDINGS AND CONCLUSIONS

In this section I will summarize the findings of this project, dividing them into the four main areas I chose to investigate. I will first present the main factors that I found to contribute to the participants' interpretation of the parents' immigration as sacrifice or abandonment. Next, I will report on the factors that seemed most important in shaping these children's representational models of self, followed by an account of what I found to be the most influential elements that formed their representational models of others. Finally, I will report on how the experience of separation influenced their emotional development.

Sacrifice or Abandonment

The first research question inquired whether children separated due to piecemeal immigration interpreted and internalized the parent's immigration as sacrifice or abandonment and which factors played a role in these children's interpretation of the parents' decision. The main findings to address the first research questions were:

The importance of contextual factors:
They were roughly classified as external or internal circumstances that led to the parents' immigration. External forces included fleeing from war and/ or from poverty. Internal forces were interpreted as parents trying to escape family conflict and pressure or an abusive relationship with a spouse or partner. Extreme poverty and hardship were the most common and the strongest reasons for the parent or parents to immigrate. All parents told these children that they were coming to the U.S. to seek a better future for the family. Such priority given to family needs and immigration due to financial strain was congruent with findings from previous research done with immigrants (Gil & Vega, 1996; Glasgow & Gouse-Sheese, 1995) and with the values of *familismo* among Latino families (Harwood, 1992). If the children were old enough to be aware and remember how poor the family was before the parents' immigration, then it was easier for these children to internalize the parents' action as a sacrifice. Children who perceived the parent's actions as an effort to flee from family conflict and abuse became more ambiguous in believing the parents and/ or caretakers. Fleeing from an abusive relationship or a broken heart presented a much greater source of conflict and anxiety for the children because it meant the enemy was now internal to the family and, in most cases, among people the children wanted to love and be close to. Finally, family cohesion and validation of the parents' explanations were helpful to avoid these children feeling rejected or abandoned.

Parents' dependability as providers:
The second factor that influenced whether the children internalized the parent's immigration as abandonment or sacrifice was associated with the parents' dependability in providing for and contacting the children while separated. Very much in line with findings reported by Glasgow and Gouse-Sheese (1995), the participants in this study also reported

that periodic contact through phone calls, letters, presents, and money was essential to validate their belief that the parents left for the benefit of the children. If these children saw in concrete ways that life was more comfortable after the parents' departure, they felt less anxious or ambivalent about the parents' true motivation to immigrate to the U.S. Moreover, if influential adults, such as surrogate parents and caretakers reinforced the children's perception of sacrifice, and if the community supported and normalized the parents' decision, it became easier for the children not to feel abandoned during the period of separation.

Role of the caretakers:

Caretakers not only took care of the children during the period of separation, but also had the task of interpreting the parents' actions and messages. The other essential role of the caretaker was that of guardian of the image and memory of the absent parent as self-sacrificing and committed to the family. These surrogate caretakers helped preserve the image of the absent parent as caring and committed to the children. The messages, beliefs, and behaviors of caretakers during the separation helped the children process and integrate their experience, and caretakers were usually well intended. However, they unintentionally sent less desirable messages to these children. Sometimes overtly, other times covertly, those adults often urged the children to suppress any feelings or expression of anger or resentment towards the absent parent. There were three main harmful messages that separated children got from their caretakers during the separation. First, children feared that any feelings of grief, loss, or resentment towards the absent parent or parents might be interpreted as selfishness and ingratitude for the parents' sacrifice. Second, by putting on a brave face and not showing their sadness, the children were in fact protecting the parents from their own sadness and frustration for having to leave the family. Now children and parents had their roles reversed, with the children being placed in the position of emotional caretakers of the parents. Thirdly, the relationship between parent and child often had a give-and-take, business quality about it. Caretakers told the children they had to study hard, behave well, respect, and love their parents because the parents were in the U.S. for their sake - so that they could have a better life, so that they could have a better future. The children were to thank and pray for the parents each time they sent them money. Sadly, children were robbed not only of the day-to-day company of the parent, but also of the experience of being loved and loving unconditionally.

Reunification, sacrifice, and the children's turn:
For many of the children interviewed for this project, there was the explicit message that, in the same way that the parents had made a sacrifice for the well-being of the children, now that these children were in the U.S., it was their turn to make sacrifices for their family. It was the children's turn to pay the parents back for the hardships they endured to bring the kids to the U.S. Most of the participants found it extremely difficult to express to their parents how unhappy they felt about being in the U.S. as they wanted to please and protect the parents and also show that they were worthy of the sacrifices the parents made. Respect and proper demeanor seem more valuable among Latinos compared to honesty and openness of communication and expression (Harwood, 1992). It could be that these values were at work in how the children interviewed for this study chose to express (or not) their true feelings and thoughts regarding the separation and reunification with their parents.

Not enough time:
Children resented the long hours parents spent at work, especially when they first arrived in the U.S. Despite the fact that they now lived in the same house, the parents again recreated the feeling of abandonment because of the amount of time they spent away from their children.

Internal Working Model of Self

The second research question investigated the impact of the prolonged separation and the participants' interpretation of that event as abandonment or sacrifice in their representational model (or internal working model) of self. Below is a description of the main findings related to question 2:

Being loved or being spoiled:
Many children equated being loved with being spoiled. The concept of being spoiled implied two conflicting messages: On the one hand the

participants saw themselves as special and deserving of being fulfilled in all their wishes and needs. On the other hand, it implied that they were getting more than they deserved, and that therefore they were being damaged in some way. According to attachment theory, a history of separation in childhood predisposes individuals to form insecure patterns of attachment. In turn, insecurely attached persons are more likely to have ambivalent and unstable feelings about their self-worth and the ability of others to provide the emotional support they need (Bowlby, 1982; Harris & Bifulco, 1991). Therefore, the participants' ambivalence could be explained by the attachment patterns developed due to a history of disruption in the relationship with their main attachment figure.

Most participants volunteered memories of caretakers cooking for them, and food was mentioned in all interviews, usually associated with feelings of being loved and cared for. Parents demonstrated their love by sending money and presents to the participants. Whereas most children mentioned how they were able to talk and play with their caretakers, when referring to their parents, they talked about respect and authority. If respect and authority constituted the core of the relationship between the participants and their parents, then one can assume that open and free communication in the family was a difficult task to achieve. Besides, when we think of authority and respect, fear rather than love is the feeling that mostly comes to mind. Therefore, one could expect that the barriers created by fear, difficulty trusting and communicating, the felt obligation of respect, and the hierarchical distance that these children felt in relation to their unfamiliar parents made the transition to their new lives a rather lonely and frightening journey. According to the report of Glasgow and Gouse-Sheese (1995), the participants in their support group for reunited adolescents also voiced frustration about the emotional distance they felt towards their biological parents, as well as anger for the felt-obligation of respect towards people they barely knew.

Marital status of parents:
All participants seemed to give much importance to the parents' marital status. They saw marital separation or having a child out of wedlock as shameful and as a reflection on their own self-worth. Children of single

parents felt inadequate and less valuable compared to their peers. For those whose parents were married and together, there was an unspoken feeling of pride. In addition, those with unmarried mothers felt more anxious and insecure about the immigration situation. They feared that if their mother or father found a new partner in the U.S. and started a new family here, there was a greater chance that they would be forgotten and would never reunite with their parent.

Trusting and Competency:
Most participants considered school and career a priority. They reported taking school seriously, and for the most part, they seemed to have goals and ambition for their future. This could indicate a healthy trust in their abilities and a secure and hopeful sense about their future. It could also suggest that they have internalized a strong sense of obligation to succeed as their payback for all the sacrifices their parents made.

Although the children interviewed said they took school seriously, most of them did quite poorly academically and their grades were below average. One can assume that as their school achievement fell below their hopes and did not match their efforts, their sense of competency and of self as able to succeed in this new society were further damaged. These findings could also relate to Blos' (1962) notion that adolescents in general tend to have an over-inflated sense of self and an unrealistically appraisal of their abilities and goals. The function of such unrealistic views is to prepare adolescents to feel able enough to begin the process of individuation from their parents. If that is the case, considering that the adolescents interviewed faced the additional burden of feeling competent in a culture they barely knew, then it would make sense that they would have to compensate for the possible sense of inadequacy by being even more unrealistic about their skills and abilities.

Finally, competency and mastery seemed to be related to having a supportive father. Many of the participants mentioned how their fathers helped them with schoolwork and encouraged them to venture in the world outside the family. Congruent with the reports on the relationship of fathers with their adolescent children (Shulman & Seiffge, 1997), adolescents perceive their father's natural inclination to be more distant in the families as an indication of their respect and support for their children's independence and ability to successfully enter the adult world.

Criticisms and disappointments:
Many participants talked about feeling immensely hurt by the parents' criticisms and their comments, once they reunited with their parents, of how the children had been spoiled by their caretakers. Most participants, if not all, felt harshly criticized by the parents and had little internal strength or external resources to protect themselves against the parents' criticisms and accusations, especially in the first and second year following their arrival.

Internal Working Model of Others

The third research question investigated the impact of the separation and its interpretation in the participants' internal working model of others. These were the main findings related to the third research question:

Explanations:
Parents often left without saying goodbye or explaining to the children why they were leaving until much later, in some cases, not until years later. That seemed to place an extra burden on the children and contribute to their view of adults as unreliable and untrustworthy. Besides failing to say goodbye to their children, as family members told the children about the parent's departure, there was often a covert message that these children were somehow responsible for their parents failing to say goodbye. Maybe because the parent could not bear the sadness at the time of departure, the children were made responsible for the parent's actions, as if they were the ones expected to contain the anxiety, grief, and distress of the parent.

Although unintentionally, caretakers often added to the children's confusion and distrust in others by lying to them about the parent's whereabouts, the expected date of return, or by keeping a deafening silence around the parents' immigration altogether. It seems that a combination of ignorance and guilt influenced how these families approached the events around the parents' departure and absence.

Parents and grandparents lacked information and understanding of how important it would be to include the children and to explain to them what was happening in the family: the need for the parents to immigrate, and their plans to leave the children in the care of relatives. Maybe because they did not know how to relay that information in a developmentally appropriate manner, they told themselves that the children would not understand or would not tolerate the stress that such information would generate. Therefore, the adults justified to themselves the cruelty of their silence by saying to themselves that the children would be better protected if kept out of the conversations altogether. It could also be that the parents were trying to protect themselves from their own sense of guilt and pressure over the need and even the desire to leave behind the problems, the past, poverty, and the children.

Fathers and Alcoholism:
Mothers were seen as sacrificing and responsible, whereas fathers, for the most part, were viewed as unruly, irresponsible children themselves. Whereas the male participants seemed to find excuses and minimized the father's behavior, the females interviewed were much less forgiving and freely expressed their resentment and anger for their father's shortcomings. It seems that males had a greater need to preserve the image of males compared to females, probably because being of the same gender. Fathers were more accessible role models for the boys interviewed compared to the girls. Finally, cultural norms and expectations could help to explain the gender differences found in this particular issue.

Mutual disappointment:
Parents, children, and life as a whole did not seem to match anybody's dreams and expectations about what would happen once the family was reunited. Participants expressed deep disappointment for how their real mother or father turned out to be, compared to their fantasies and expectations about their parents and life in the U.S. These findings were congruent with the report of Glasgow & Gouse-Sheese (1995) on that group of adolescents and their experience of reunification with their parents.

Separation and Emotional Development

The fourth research question focused on separation in childhood and its impact in emotional development and well-being of the participants. These are the most significant findings in addressing this question:

Feeling disconnected:
When asked how they thought the prolonged separation had affected them, many participants conveyed the feeling of a loss that would never be repaired. They also seemed to feel they should only rely on themselves for support and to resolve difficulties. Many felt isolated and feared that seeking help would be interpreted as a sign of weakness, and there was a general sense of hopeless and sadness in the participants' presentation, even though at times they showed a brave face. Some of these children reported feeling distant or disconnected from others and doubted their own ability to feel love for others.

For many of the participants, joining the parents in the U.S. was a journey full of hopes and expectations. For many of these children it seemed to be their opportunity to make up for the losses they suffered in the past. However, as they arrived and watched the relationship fall short of their dreams, they once again were faced with further deprivation. Many of the participants felt that the relationship with their parents would never recover from the lost time and lost connection. Besides, parents and children lacked a shared history, memories, and traditions. They felt awkward and unable to re-engage once the family reunited.

Some of the participants, however, seemed to find a way to reconnect to the parents. As these children started to relate to their parents more as adults and peers, they felt more accepting of and accepted by the parents. For some of the participants, becoming parents themselves seemed to make it easier to reconnect to their own parents. For others, starting to take on the role of workers and wage earners represented the equalizer they needed to finally be able to get along. It seems that as they entered the late or post adolescent phase of development (Blos, 1962; Gemelli, 1997) they were now faced with the task of developing their own careers and families. Therefore, these children were better able to have a more realistic appraisal of their relationship with their parents and to become more accepting of life's limitations and constraints.

Pride and a good upbringing:
Some participants saw many advantages in being raised in Latin America and being brought up by their grandmothers. They saw themselves as polite and respectful, highly valued traits in the Latino culture (Gil & Vega, 1996). Many felt happy to think of how proud their caretakers were with the kind of young men and women they turned out to be. Others felt proud of their parents for the efforts that they made to succeed in this country.

Covert feelings:
The analysis of the sand trays provided information about covert feelings and internal processes the participants experienced. Many sand trays revealed symptoms of depression and anxiety in the sandplayers, and suggested these children's regrets about the relocation to the U.S. Another feature of many of the trays was the participants' desire to help the parents or the caretakers. These children also seemed more emotionally fulfilled in their relationships with caretakers compared to the parents. Patterns of the sand trays seemed to differentiate participants that reported less distress about their life history and relationship with caretakers or parents compared to those with more disturbed affect, and adjustment difficulties. Number of miniatures used, range of categories of these miniatures, approach of the task of the construction of sand tray, and patterns of maps of the sand trays showed many commonalties with research done using sand trays (Rodgers-Mitchell & Friedman, 1994).

IMPLICATIONS FOR PRACTITIONERS

In the process of conducting this research project, I believe I increased my ability and effectiveness to work with families with a history of piecemeal immigration and prolonged separation. Hopefully, this report will also help inform other counselors, therapists, and educators working with these families and children. The stories and voice of the participants helped me understand their experiences. Based on the findings and results of this study, I present below a list of recommendations for practitioners to help these families and children improve their ability to face the challenges ahead of them.

<u>Open, frequent, accepting, and empathic communication:</u>
This includes helping these families inform and include the children in their decision-making process prior to immigration, saying their good-byes and being honest about plans to return, timelines, and reasons for the immigration. Practitioners should guide and encourage parents and caretakers to deliver this information in a developmentally appropriate manner, and to give full permission for these children to express and voice their feelings, questions, and fears related to the separation process. If necessary, professionals working with this population should help these children understand and interpret their internal state by prompting possible feelings and cognition these children might be experiencing. Empathy and permissiveness regarding the full range of feelings that these children might be experiencing should also be clearly communicated. Of course many practitioners do not have access to these families prior to immigration. One possible way to help these families would be to educate the parents about the importance of clear and honest communication and encourage them to contact their children as soon as possible and repair any behaviors that could be harmful in the future. For example, if the parent left without saying goodbye, then counselors could encourage these parents to call the child and explain the circumstances, and *apologize* for the inappropriate behavior. Sending an apology card or something concrete that the child can refer to periodically should also be suggested.

During the period of separation, keeping frequent contact with these children should be encouraged. Phone calls, pictures, letters, frequent gifts and mementos should be sent as frequently as conditions allow. Parents should be encouraged to be honest about their financial condition so that children do not build unrealistic expectations about the parents' economic resources.

Upon arrival of these children, parents should be encouraged to take time off work, if at all possible, and most importantly, begin the process of rebuilding the dialogue and the relationship with their children. Practitioners should help parents set clear but kind boundaries and expectations, and again build an accepting and empathic attitude regarding the expression of the range of feelings the family might be experiencing.

Avoiding competition with and criticism of previous caretakers:
Parents should be prepared to expect that the children will grieve the loss of the caretaker upon arrival in the U.S. They should be encouraged to allow these children to grieve the loss of the caretaker freely, without feeling that by doing so they are being ungrateful to their parents. Parents should also be assured of the importance of encouraging their children to continue contact with their previous caretakers and to avoid at all costs placing these children in a position where they feel pressured to choose between the surrogate families and their biological families. For blended families, this should also apply to the new members of these families and their half-sibling.

Continuity of care:
Ideally, the children were placed in the care of a kind caretaker during the period of separation and did not experience multiple changes in caretaking arrangements. However, circumstances are often not ideal. If discontinuity and changes in caretaking arrangements occurred, professionals involved with these families should consider evaluating the child for a referral to assess possible trauma, abuse, and other psychological problems.

Behaviors of unconditional love:
Many children with a history of separation seem to lack the opportunity to experience the feeling of being loved unconditionally by their parents. Parents should be educated about behaviors that could facilitate the recovery of such feelings and encouraged to engage in those behaviors as often as possible. Cooking and feeding seem to be one of those behaviors, for example. Playing, talking and "joking-around" were also mentioned by the participants in this project as a sign that they were loved and had a close relationship with their parents or caretakers.

Education, referral and treatment:
Education of families, parents, and children with a history of piecemeal immigration and prolonged separation is essential. That could be approached and achieved in different ways and settings. Discussion

groups at schools, churches, community centers, human services, and mental health centers targeted to families and professionals working with these populations could greatly improve the functioning of these families and individuals. However, assessment and appropriate referrals should also be part of the strategy and plan when working with this population. After all, as a group, these children are at increase risk of developing symptoms of mental illness compared to children who did not experience separation in childhood (Masser, 1992). A full history to assess trauma, abuse, and neglect should also be considered. These families also have a greater chance to experience conflict and discord that could impair emotional growth and optimum functioning. Alcohol and drug use of the parent (particularly the father) should be considered and assessed.

RECOMMENDATIONS FOR FUTURE RESEARCH

In approaching this project, I made a conscious decision to focus on attachment theory as I tried to understand how the participants in this study interpreted the world around them. This seemed a natural decision because aside from my personal interest in that theoretical model, it seemed most appropriate for exploring this topic. However, such choice does not imply in any way that attachment should be the only construct that could inform and guide the study of this population and set of life events. Family systems theory and human development theory, for example, could provide alternative explanations for the feelings, cognition, and behavior patterns observed in individuals with a similar life history. Therefore, although it is beyond the scope of this project to elaborate on these theories and constructs, we would greatly benefit from research that used alternative lenses to understand the topic investigated in this study. Below is a proposed list of recommendations for future research:

1. Investigate the process of prolonged separation and reunification among immigrant families using other theoretical approaches and perspectives, such as family systems theory, or cognitive theory.

2. Investigate the role of separation and reunification in the context of immigration and the development of specific clusters of mental illness, particularly the mood disorders, such as depression, the anxiety disorders (including posttraumatic stress disorder), and conduct disorders.

3. Conduct a larger and more comprehensive study, looking at variables such as the effect of trauma and war-related issues compared to other life experiences in this population. Such study could allow for the presentation of sets of variables and circumstances that might determine better adjustment to the reunification with biological parents.

4. Conduct a study that includes interviews with the parents and their children separated during the process of immigration. The interplay of the parents' psychological health, personality traits, and the presence or absence of mental illness could be an important aspect to better understand not only issues around the separation, but most importantly, to better understand the role it plays in the characteristics of the reunification process.

5. Investigate the impact of prolonged separation due to immigration on academic performance and achievement.

6. Conduct studies with other cultural groups with a similar pattern of immigration, such as people from the Middle East, Africa, and Asia to tease what elements of the results might be explained by cultural differences compared to universal traits.

7. Conduct longitudinal studies to investigate the long-term impact of prolonged separation from parents.

8. Conduct cross-generational studies to investigate cross generational attachment patterns among this population.

9. Conduct research to investigate the impact and effects of intervention upon reunification of these children with their parent or parents.

CONCLUSIONS

Piecemeal patterns of immigration continue to prevail among Latinos, and particularly among the poor. That means a history of prolonged separation and discontinuity of attachment for their children. How the event is interpreted by these children, the nuances of messages sent by parents and caretakers, particular circumstances and characteristics of relationships following the reunification, as well as individual differences, all play an important role in whether these families will succeed once they reunite. These elements will also influence how these children will relate to others, how they will see themselves, how safe and welcoming they will perceive their world, and how they will meet developmental tasks and life challenges. Ignorance plays an important role in this whole process. Families and the community lack information, knowledge, experience, and insight to guide the process of separation and reunification, increasing the distress in all involved. The ending result is little or no discussion about feelings and concerns among family members. Recognizing and validating these families feelings, fears, and needs can help them integrate their experience and rebuild broken relationships. Professionals involved with Latino children, such as teachers and mental health professionals, can be instrumental in facilitating the adjustment process for these families. Finally, further investigation and research on this topic can greatly benefit not only Latino immigrants, but other immigrants and refugees that share a similar life history.

APPENDIX A: INTERVIEW GUIDE

INSTRUMENT: INTERVIEW GUIDE

FIRST INTERVIEW SESSION:

Could you orient me to your early family life? Who was part of your family as you were growing up? Did you always live together? Did you move around a lot? Where were you born? Who would you say raised you?

INDIVIDUAL STORIES
>   Can you take me back to the days just before your Mother/Father departure to the U.S.?
>   The day of the departure?
>   The weeks and months following their immigration?
>   When you were a child (or at age X), what kind of stories did you tell yourself about the reason why your parents came to the U.S.?
>   What kinds of feelings do you remember having as you thought of them leaving?
>   How would you describe your relationship with your Mother/Father before age …(stated age at onset of separation)?
>   Can you describe an event that illustrates your relationship with your mother/father as … (adjective used by participant to describe relationship)?

FAMILY STORIES
>   What do you remember your grandmother (or other caretaker during separation) telling you about your Mother/Father? About their decision to come to the U.S.?

CULTURAL STORIES
>   Did you talk about Mother/Father at school? With friends? What did you tell them about your Mother/Father leaving? What was their response?

LIFE/ RELATIONSHIPS DURING SEPARATION

How would you describe your relationship with your grandmother/ grandfather (or main caretaker) from ages .... to ....(stated age of separation)?

Can you describe an event that illustrates the relationship with grandmother/ grandfather as ...(adjective used by participant to describe relationship)?

Interviewer will then direct participant to the construction of a scene using miniatures and a box filled with sand.

"Now let me show you this wooden tray filled with sand. When I pull the sand away you can see that the bottom of the box is painted blue, and some people think of it as a way to represent water. Now, on these shelves there are miniatures of things commonly found in the world: Wild and farm animals, transportation vehicles, structures, such as houses, bridges, and fences, plants, like trees, and flowers, mythological figures, and human figures. Using as many or as few miniatures as you like, I'd like you to build a world in the sand tray. There is some water here also, if you'd like to Use it to wet the sand. Take your time, while I just sit here.

Once the scene is completed, the interviewer may ask some clarifying questions to the participant, without, however, attempting to give meaning or offer interpretations to any aspects of the construction. She will also ask what the title of that work should be and from what angle should the photograph be taken. Any clarification and discussion about the final product will remain at a symbolic level, and the researcher will only use images and words that were used by the participant. This is a very non-directive approach, even though a structured way to interpret the process and ending result will be applied.

The dialogue about the tray will also be audiotape and transcribed. Participants will be reminded that a copy of the picture can be provided to the participant, if he or she so wishes.

INSTRUMENT: INTERVIEW GUIDE

SECOND INTERVIEW SESSION:

Open the interview by briefly summarizing the topic discussed in the previous session and asking whether participant has thought about anything he or she would like to talk about that was left out or needed further explanation/ processing, debriefing, etc.

IMPACT ON THE RELATIONSHIP WITH MOTHER/ FATHER

Now, as a young man/ woman, how do you see your parents' motives to come to the U.S.?

What kinds of feelings do you have now as you think back to that time you were separated?

How would you describe your relationship with your Mother/Father currently?

Can you describe an event that illustrates your relationship with your mother/father as ... (adjective used by participant to describe relationship)?

IMPACT ON PERSONAL DEVELOPMENT

How do you think the separation from your mother/ father affected your personal development?

IMPACT ON OTHER IMPORTANT RELATIONSHIPS

Who are you close to now?

Can you give me three adjectives to describe your relationship with X (person mentioned above)?

Could you tell me about a specific memory that would illustrate the relationship as ... (adjective used by participant to describe relationship)?

How is your relationship with your grandmother/ grandfather (or other stable caretaker during the period of separation) currently?

How would you describe your relationship with boyfriends/ girlfriends? Are you dating anybody? Can you tell me a bit about your love life at this time?

ADJUSTING TO LIFE IN THE U.S.

Can you describe the first couple weeks as you arrived in the U.S.? What kinds of feelings and thoughts did you experience?

How was your relationship with your mother? Father? Stepfather? _ siblings? Can you tell me a story that illustrates what you just said?

How were the first weeks of going to school in the U.S.? Can you tell me an event that serves as an example of what you just said?

LOOKING AT THE FUTURE

What are your plans for the future?

Do you think of getting married or having children in the future?

What country would you like to live if you could just choose whichever one you would like? Why X country?

Any career plans?

ATTACHMENT STYLE CHECKLIST:

I would like you to choose from these three statements, the one that best describes your feelings:

1. I find it relatively easy to get close to others and I am comfortable depending on them. I don't often worry about being abandoned or about someone getting too close to me. (Secure type).

2. I am somewhat uncomfortable being close to others; I find it difficult to trust them completely, difficult to allow myself to depend on them, I am nervous when anyone gets too close, and often, love partners want me to be more intimate than I feel comfortable being (Avoidant type).

3. I find that others are reluctant to get as close as I would like. I often worry that my partner doesn't really love me or won't want to stay with me. I want to get very close to my partner, and this sometimes scares people away (Anxious/ambivalent type).

Hazan & Shaver, 1987.

Now, very much like last time, I would like to ask you to build another world using the miniatures and sand tray, if you would. As you remember, if you pull the sand away you can see that the bottom of the box is painted blue, and can represent water. And here are the different miniatures; the wild and farm animals, transportation, structures, plant life, human figures and mythological figures. Use as many or as few miniatures as you'd like, while I will just sit here in the corner. And you can also use water, of course.

Once again, as the scene is completed, the processing will follow very much the same guidelines used in the previous interview session.

APPENDIX B: PHOTOGRAPHS OF THE SAND TRAYS

Jorge: Sand tray 1

Jorge: Sand tray 2

Suzana: Sand tray 1

Suzana: Sand tray 2

Isabella: Sand tray 1

Isabella: Sand tray 2

Rita: Sand trays 1

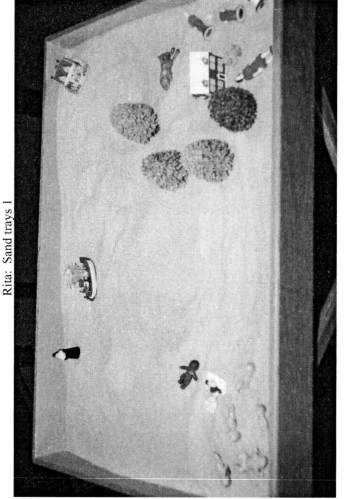

Rita: Sand tray 2

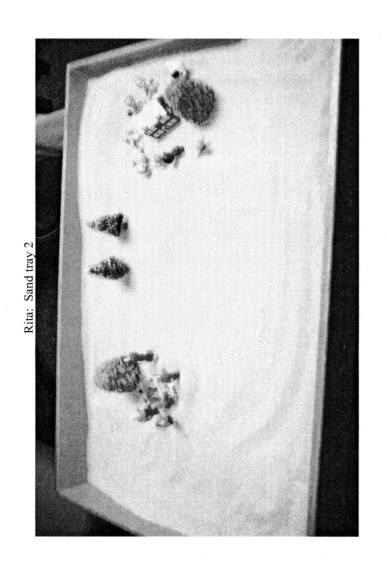

Luis: Sand tray 1

Luis: Sand tray 2

Carla:　Sand tray 1

Carla: Sand tray 2

Alex: Sand tray 1

Alex: Sand tray 2

APPENDIX C: SAND TRAY ANALYSIS PROTOCOL

Ryce-Menuhin Mapping of Sand Trays (11)

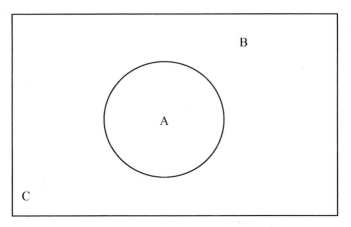

Figure 1. Most usual order builders choose in building a sand tray, often called the classical approach.

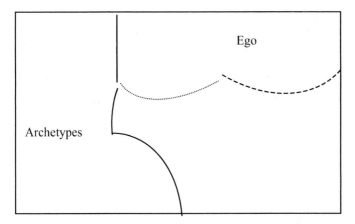

Figure 2. Approximation of where the ego and archetype materials are most likely to appear.

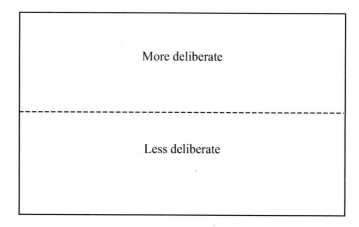

Figure 3. Placement of objects in relation to the body of the builder. Upper half receives a more deliberate attention from the builder

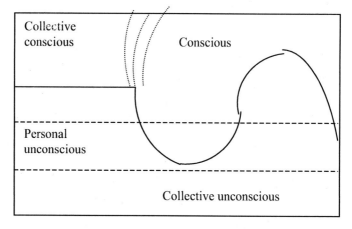

Figure 4. When personal and collective unconscious are present in the sand tray, they often assume this organization.

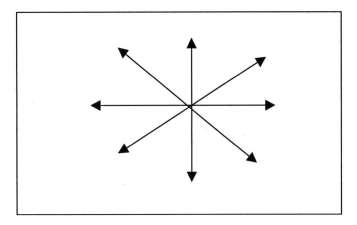

Figure 5. Arrows can refer to relations of direction, complementarity, direct opposites, complimentary opposites, color balances, dynamic of movement of objects.

Figure 6. The double lines are often used to defend against threatening material

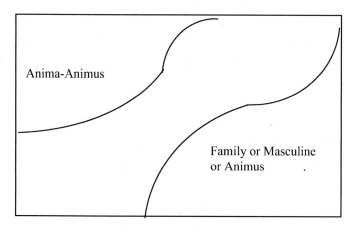

Figure 7. Family constellations often occur in the lower right-hand corner. Anima and Animus images often occur in the upper left-hand corner of the sand tray.

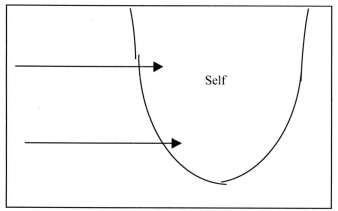

Figure 8. True manifestation of the self may be represented in the center, with dynamic action with or against the self often emanating from the left side.

APPENDIX C: SAND TRAY ANALYSIS PROTOCOL
Erica Method of Sand Tray Analysis

Miniatures are arranged in an open shelf divided by categories:
1. People and humanoid life forms
2. Animals
3. Plant life
4. Minerals
5. Environments or structures
6. Miscellaneous

Analysis based on two levels of reading:

A. Formal aspects of the construction:
1. Choice and treatment of the sand
2. Number of miniatures used
3. Developmental level of construction
4. Changes and corrections
5. Order of construction and choice of miniatures
6. Time limits
7. Verbalization
8. Level of composition:
   (a) Configuration
   (b) Simple categorization
   (c) Juxtaposition
   (d) Conventional grouping
   (e) Meaningful scene
   (f) Atypical composition

B. Content analysis:
1. Analysis of predominant themes,
2. Approach to the task (Level of motivation, self-doubt, anxiety, fear, etc.)
3. Verbalizations during task
4. Story or explanations given about choices or construction
5. Title chosen for the construction

APPENDIX D: SAMPLE CODED INTERVIEW SEGMENT

R –And how often did you see your mother? Did she ever go visit you?	
S – I was 2... When I was 6 years old... 6 years later I met her for the first time [laughs] ... and it was so funny because they kept showing me pictures but I never really actually see her, you know, So, they were all surprised because if you have never actually seen someone .. to see them is different... you know, [high pitch], the picture from a person is different sometimes. Like I saw her... I will never forget. She was wearing ... the first, first time she went, if I am not mistaken, she was wearing a black dress and a she looked like a [laughs] she looked like a turkey.... [laughs]. She was wearing a black dress and an overcoat ... I don't know how you call it... and she had a pin right here [showing the collar bone area], but it looked like.. Man, I don't know how to explain it..	Good quote Mother as Damaged.
And then I started crying, I was like... that is my MOM... My aunt was carrying me, that is my mom, that is my mom, and then she looked at me and I started crying, and they were like... Oh, my God, she recognized her mom, and I kept telling my grandma, cause by then my aunt gave me to my grandma, so that she could carry me, and I was... that is my mom, that is my mom, and then there were bars, like she was in jail, because of immigration - she had to pass all that and then she would hold my hand, and she would not let me go... she would not let go of my hand. And then I met her... I hugged her... I was, my mom, it is like being through like, someone you've never seen, and I was like... Uau, my mom, you know... and then... It was [hesitation in the voice] fine until, like, you know... they are ... you are not going to live with them, and they are so nice to you.... And everything... The only thing that I... she was loud.... We were like... be quiet, you know... don't talk so loud... Like, if she wanted us to do something – me and my cousin, she would scream -	Self as hero Metaphor Mother as damaged

and we would say, don't scream, mama, don't scream... they are not used to people screaming at them... If you come, talk to them calmly and nicely... and she would go [pretending she is screaming, but in a buffered voice]... well, that is the way I talk... and I am like.... They don't like it... it irritates them, you know [higher pitch]... if you are not used to something it is hard... So she ... I mean, it was fine, you know...	Mother as damaged/ Culture as damaged
And there were plenty of things that she would do, like, 'cause she came for mothers' day, in March ?.. May, May. And then I would go to school and she would be so loud... I would be in the bus, and the bus came to pick us up in front of each kid's house... It is different from here, where you go to a bus stop place.. No, the bust came to <u>your house</u>, and your parents would put you in the bus. So sometimes I would stay and wait for the bus, and then she would <u>scream</u>, like... I would go to say bye to her, and she would scream BYE, HONEY... and I would not understand the HONEY part, and the kids would say, What is your mom saying? BYE? I don't know, like tchau, HONEY? I didn't know... They teach you the basic, like, Hi, Hello, Bye... and then she would say, bye honey... And the kids would say "is that your mom?" Because they were used to seeing my grandma always outside and my friends knew all my family... and they would be like... is that your mom who came from the United States? Because over there, to people, the United States is the richest country, and you get so many lectures... and I was like... hum, you know, it was just so funny, because people would be like... UAU, you know...	Mother as hero
R – What do you think they meant with "uau"?	
S - Like, they used to think that .... Because my aunt and my mom worked so hard to build a house... Because we had like, a two-story house, it has 4	Sacrifice

bathrooms and everything, you know... our house... So they used to be... you rich little spoiled girl who had everything... Whom my parents were in the United States... They used to think that my mom was <u>wealthy and rich</u>. Even though I used to think that. I used to think, Uau, my mom is rich, she is a .. woman Why? Because of all the money she was spending ... but I never knew the truth... that she lived in a little apartment, you know... Uncomfortable... Because over there ... See because this is what the parents don't tell you... They never show you the real thing, like how they suffer... or anything. So, how can you know? I would think that I used to think that she was here with another husband, you know... I used to think that she never loved me, that she left me there [participant stars to cry]. And I kind of resent her for that... but I really, because I mean, she did me a favor, because then maybe I would suffer with her, and not have the best time with my grandma.. my aunt...	Love= Spoiled Self as Damaged Sacrifice Vs. Abandonm ent

APPENDIX E: SAMPLE SAND TRAY ANALYSIS
Erica Method of Sand Tray Analysis

Jorge:
SAND TRAY 1// *SAND TRAY 2*

Categories:

1. People and humanoid figures –   1 MAN, 1 WOMAN, 1 FIGHTER// *NO HUMANS. ONE GREEN MAN*
2. Animals - FARM ANIMALS, HUGE DOG, SNAKES, PIGS, HORSES// *COWS, PIGS, DINOSAURS, BIRDS*
3. Plant life – FEW TREES. *MORE TREES THAN IN TRAY 1. HUGE DEAD TRUNK*
4. Minerals – WATER, RIVER// *NOTHING*
5. Environments or structures – FENCES, TRUCKS, CARS, BOATS, HOUSE, WELL// *WELL*
6. Miscellaneous -

Formal aspects of the construction:

1. Choice and treatment of the sand – CAREFUL, THOUGHTFUL, DELIBERATE// *ALSO CAREFUL AND DELIBERATE*
2. Number of miniatures used – 50// *42*
3. Developmental level of construction – WITHIN NORMAL LIMITS (WNL)// *WITHIN NORMAL LIMITS (WNL)*
4. Changes and corrections – NONE – *NONE*
5. Order of construction and choice of miniatures – HOUSE, HORSES, FENCES, COWS, RIVER, CARS, TREES// *FENCES, TREES, HOUSE/BARN, WELL, COWS*
6. Time limits – WNL (10 TO 15")// *WNL (15")*
7. Verbalization – ASKS PERMISSION TO USE MINIATURES REPEATEDLY [PARALLEL PROCESS TO NEEDING OTHERS TO HELP CONTAIN SELF?]; ASKS FOR SPECIFIC MINIATURES HE CAN'T FIND (SUCH AS A BRIDGE) [PARALLEL PROCESS TO EXPECTATION THAT NEEDS WILL NOT BE FULFILLED?]// *ASKS PERMISSION TO USE MINIATURES ONLY 2 TIMES. LESS VERBALIZATION THAN DURING FIRST TRAY*

8. Level of composition
   a. Configuration – WNL// *WNL*
   b. Simple categorization – YES// *YES*
   c. Juxtaposition – 3// *1*
   d. Conventional grouping – YES// *YES*
   e. Meaningful scene – YES// *YES*
   f. Atypical composition – NO// *SOMEWHAT*

Content analysis:

1. Analysis of predominant themes – LIFE IN EL SALVADOR, COWS AND HORSES, UNCLE, ACTIVITIES// *BOUNDARIES BUILT WITH FENCES, TREE-LINES, ROAD FOR THE TRUCK*

2. Approach to the task (Level of motivation, self-doubt, anxiety, fear, etc.) – COMMITTED, INVOLVED, MOTIVATED, SOMEWHAT ANXIOUS AS ASKED QUESTIONS AND HELP TO SET UP BOUNDARIES AND RULES, CAREFUL HANDLING OF THE SAND// *CAREFUL CHOICE AND DELIBERATE PLACEMENT OF THE MINIATURES, CALM APPROACH TO TASK, VERY INVOLVED AND ABSORBED DURING TASK, CREATIVE AND INNOVATIVE USE OF MATERIAL, MODIFIES MATERIALS TO MEET NEEDS, SEEMS PLEASED WITH RESULTS, PROUD OF SELF ND TRAY*

3. Verbalizations during task – NONE, BUT FOR WHEN ASKING PERMISSION TO USE MINIATURES// *NONE*

4. Story or explanations given about choices or construction – SAYS IT REPRESENTS HIS HOUSE AND LIFE STYLE IN EL SALVADOR// *ONLY LITERAL DESCRIPTION OF GROUPINGS*

5. Title chosen for the construction – "WHERE I LIVED, WHERE I GREW UP// *INAUDIBLE.*

Ryce-Menuhin Mapping of the Sand Trays

Jorge: Tray 1, Figure 3

More Deliberate

Orderly fenced in, compartmentalized aspects of the self: house, family, guarded by big, loyal dog, and horses (sexuality) well-fenced in? Cows are the idilic life in the past/ childhood and horses as the buding sexuality? animal impulses vs. loyal cows? Family and home as a divided?

Less Deliberate

Fighter/ fighting - Bridge: Need to be a strong, concrete truck to be able to overcome need for nurturance? Cars moving to the left = moving towards the past? River = nurturance. Boat = loosing oneself; Woman on the boat/ falling in love? At the mercy of destiny? Snakes = sexuality?

Jorge: Tray 2, Figure 3

More Deliberate

Cows are the ones fenced in now. Same position as in tray 1 (past). All animals are farm/ tame animals. House/ Barn right in the middle of conscious/ unconscious, but also in the past. Past seems fenced in and in the future, a big, dead, empty trunk?? No human figures, only green humanoid figure.

Less Deliberate

Trees are equally distributed. Primitive animals in the lower part, future location only. Dinosaurs are fenced out, (under control?). Opposite, a well (nurturance?), but also in the location for past.

Jorge: Tray 1, Figure 8

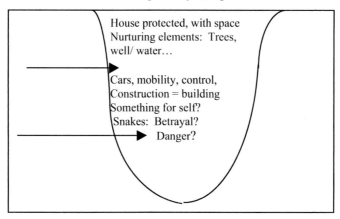

House protected, with space
Nurturing elements: Trees,
well/ water...

Cars, mobility, control,
Construction = building
Something for self?
Snakes: Betrayal?
Danger?

Jorge: Tray 2, Figure 8

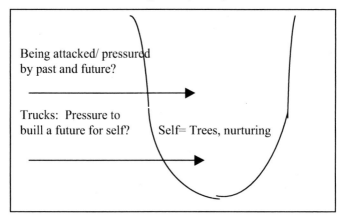

Being attacked/ pressured
by past and future?

Trucks: Pressure to
buill a future for self?

Self= Trees, nurturing

NOTES

(1) Members of the nuclear family immigrate at separate times, sometimes years apart. Most commonly, mother, father, or both immigrate first and a few years later send for their children

(2) Anaclitic depression is a term used to describe severely depressed babies who are non-reactive and in some extreme cases, present "failure to thrive" (or arrested physical development) as a symptom.

(3) The MMPI is a widely accepted personality inventory, used mostly for research, diagnostic, and treatment purposes.

(4) For further description of the Strange Situation please refer to Aisnworth, Blehar, Waters, & Wall (1978), Patterns of Attachment: A Psychological Study of the Strange Situation, Hillsdale, NJ: Erlbaum.

(5) For further information on concepts of collective and personal unconscious, please refer to chapters 1 and 3 of *Man and his Symbols* (1968), by Carl Jung (Ed.) and other work on Jungian Psychology.

(6) Central and South American civilians who rebelled against the government and armed forces.

(7) Refers to immigrants who do not have a work permit or residency papers. Their stay in the U.S. is illegal.

(8) Free nodes are non-hierarchical coding categories.

(9) Tree nodes are hierarchical coding categories.

(10) According to object-relations theory, transitional objects are objects that help keep the memory of the absent mother alive at a developmental stage when infants have not yet internalized the image of the mother.

(11) Ryce-Minuhin analyzed over 1,000 sand trays and arrived at these 8 basic configurations. However, the nature of his assertions and conclusions is merely speculative at this time. It serves here the purpose of a general guide for speculation rather than a proven and true method of analysis.

REFERENCES

Adam, K. S. (1982). Loss, suicide, and attachment. In *The Place of Attachment in Human Behavior.* C. M. Parker & J. Stevenson-Hinde (Eds.). N. Y.: Basic Books.

Adam, K. (1994). Suicidal behavior and attachment: A developmental model. In *Attachment in Adults: A Clinical Perspective.* M. Sperling & W. Berman (Eds.). New York: Guilford Press.

Aisnworth, M.D., Blehar, Waters, & Wall (1978). *Patterns of Attachment: A Psychological study of the Strange Situation,* Hillsdale, NJ: Erlbaum.

Ainsworth, M. D. (1984). Attachment across the life cycle. *Bulletin of New York Academy of Medicine, 61* (9), 792- 812.

Ainsworth, M. D. (1991). Attachments and other affectional bonds across the life cycle. In *Attachment Across the Life Cycle.* C. Murray-Parkes, J. Stevenson-Hinde and P. Mark. (Eds.) London: Tavistock/ Routledge.

American Psychiatric Association. (1994). *Diagnostic and Statistical Manual of Mental Disorders* (4th. ed.). Washington, DC: Author.

Arcia, E. & Johnson, A. (1998). When respect means to obey: Immigrant Mexican mothers' values for their children. *Journal of Child and Family Studies, 7 (1),* 79-95.

Arnold, E. (1997). Issues of reunification of migrant West Indian children in the United Kingdom. In J. L. Roopnarine and J. Brown. *Caribbean Families: Diversity Among Ethnic Groups.* Greenwich, CT: Ablex Publishing Corporation.

Arroyo, W. (1997). Central American children. In G. Johnson-Powel, J. Yamamoto, G. E. Wyatt, and W. Arroyo. *Transcultural Child Development.* New York: John Wiley & Sons, Inc.

Baptiste, Jr., D. A.(1990). The treatment of adolescents and their families in cultural transition: Issues and recommendations. *Contemporary Family Therapy, 12*(1), 3-22.

Bartholomew, K. (1990). Avoidance of intimacy: An attachment perspective. *Journal of Social and Personal Relationships, 7*, 147-178.

Bates, J. E. & Bayles, K. (1988). Attachment and the development of behavior problems. In *Clinical Implications of Attachment.* Ed. Jay Belsky. New Jersey: Lawrence Erlbaum.

Benoit, D. & Parker, K. (1994). Stability and transmission of attachment across three generations. *Child Development, 65*, 1444-1456.

Berman, W. & Sperling, M. (1994). The structure and function of adult attachment. In *Attachment in Adults: A Clinical Perspective.* M. Sperling & W. Berman (Eds.). New York: Guilford Press.

Blatt, S. J. & Blass, R.B. (1990). Attachment and separateness: A dialectical model of the products and processes of development throughout a life cycle. *Psychoanalytic Study of the Child, 45*, 107-127.

Blos, P. (1962). *On Adolescence.* New York: Free Press.

Blos, P. (1967). The second individuation process of adolescence. *Psychoanalytic Study of the Child, 22,* 162-186.

Blos, P. (1971). The child analyst looks at the young adolescent. *Daedalus, 100,* 961-978.

Bowlby, J. (1973). *Attachment and Loss: Volume II Separation.* New York: Basic Books.

Bowlby, J. (1980). *Attachment and Loss: Volume III Loss.* New York: Basic Books.

Bowlby, J. (1982). *Attachment and Loss: Volume I Attachment* (2nd. Ed.) New York: Basic Books.

Bowlby, 1988. *A Secure Base: Parent-Child Attachment and Human Development.* New York: Basic Books.

Bowyer, L. R. (1970). *The Lowenfeld World Technique.* Oxford: Pergamon Press.

Brennan, K. A. & Shaver, P. R. (1995). Dimensions of adult attachment, affect regulation, and romantic relationship functioning. *Personality and Social Psychology Bulletin, 21*, 267-283.

Brown, G. W. (1982). Early loss and depression. In *The Place of Attachment in Human Behavior.* C. M. Parkers & J. Stevenson-Hinde (Eds.). N. Y.: Basic Books.

Buhler, C. (1952). National differences in the World Test projective patterns. *Journal of Projective Techniques, 16*(1), 42-55.

Cafferty, P.S.J. & Engstrom, D.W. (2000). *Hispanics in the United States: And Agenda for the Twenty-First Century.* New Brunswick, N.J.: Transaction Publishers.

Coffey, A. & Atkinson, P. (1996). *Making Sense of Qualitative Data.* Thousand Oaks, CA: Sage Publications.

Colin, V. L. (1996b). *Human Attachment.* Philadelphia: Temple University Press.

Collins, W.A. & Luebker, C. (1991). *Change in parent-child relationships: Bilateral Processes in the transition to adolescence.* Paper presented at the Meeting of the International Society for the Study of Behavioral Development (July), Minneapolis, MN.

Cooper, V. (1990). Adolescent rhymes and reason: A Kleinian perspective. *Melanie Klein and Object Relations, 8* (2), 77-99.

Das Eiden, R.; Teti, D. M.; & Corns, K. M. (1995). Maternal working models of attachment, marital adjustment, and the parent-child relationship. *Child Development, 66*, 1504-1518.

DeHass, M.A., Bakermans-Kranenburg, M.J. & Van Ijzendoorn, M.H. (1994). The Adult Attachmen Interview and questionnaires for attachment style, temperament, and memories of parental behavior. *Journal of Genetic Psychology, 155*, 471-486.

Feeney, J. & Noller, P. (1996). *Adult Attachment.* Thousand Oaks, CA: Sage.

Fisher, L. K. (1950a). The World Test. In W. Wolf (Ed.) *Personality Symposia on Topical Issues: Projective and Expressive Methods of Personality Investigation ("Diagnosis"),* New York: Grune & Stratton.

Freeberg, A. L. & Stein, C. H., 1996. Felt obligation towards parents in Mexican-American and Anglo-American young adults. *Journal of Social and Personal Relationships, 13*(3), 457-471.

Gemelli, R. (1996). *Normal Child and Adolescent Development.* Washington, D.C.: American Psychiatric Press, Inc.

George, C., Kaplan, N., & Main, M. (1996). Adult Attachment Interview. Unpublished Manuscript, Department of Psychology, University of California, Berkley (Third Edition).

Gil, A. & Vega, W. A. (1996). Two different worlds: Acculturation stress and adaptation among Cuban and Nicaraguan families. *Journal of Social and Personal Relationships, 13*(3), 435-456.

Gilad, L. (1990). Refugees in Newfoundland: Families after flight. *Journal of Comparative Family Studies, 21*(3), 379-396.

Glasgow, G. F. & Gouse-Sheese, J. (1995). Themes of rejection and abandonment in group work with Caribbean adolescents. *Social Work with Groups, 17*(4), 3-27.

Greenberg, M. T. & Speltz, M. L. (1988). Attachment and the ontogeny of conduct problems. In *Clinical Implications of Attachment.* Ed. Jay Belsky. New Jersey: Lawrence Erlbaum.

Grossman, K., Grossman, K.E., Spangler, G., Suess, G., & Unzner, L. (1985). Maternal sensitivity and newborns' orientation responses as related to quality of attachment in Northern Germany. In I. Bretherton and E. Waters (Eds.). *Growing points of attachment theory and research, Monographs of the Society for Research in Child Development, 50*(1-2, Serial number 209), 276-297.

Grossman, K. E. & Grossmann, K. (1990). The wider concept of attachment in cross-cultural research. *Human Development, 33*(31), 31-47.

Guerra, F. A. (1999). *Emerging Health issues for children in immigrant families.* Paper presented at the Congressional Hispanic Caucus on "America's Children, America's Future, The Health and Well-Being of Children in Immigrant Families: New Findings", sponsored by the Population Resource Center, Washington DC.

Harris, T. & Bifulco, A. (1991). Loss of parent in childhood, attachment style, and depression in adulthood. In *Attachment Across the Life Cycle.* C. Murray-Parkes, J. Stevenson-Hinde and P. Mark. (Eds.) London: Tavistock/ Routledge.

Harwood, R. (1992). The influence of culturally derived values on Anglo and Puerto Rican mothers' perceptions of attachment behavior. *Child Development, 63*, 822-839.

Hazan, C. & Shaver, P. R. (1987). Romantic love conceptualization and attachment process. *Journal of Personality and Social Psychology, 52*, 511-524.

Hazan, C. & Shaver, P. R. (1990). Love and work: An attachment-theoretical perspective. *Journal of Personality and Social Psychology, 59*, 270-280.

Hernandez, D., & Darke, K. (1999). Socioeconomic and demographic risk factors and resources among children in immigrant and native born families. In Donald J. Hernandez, (Ed), *Children of Immigrants: Health, Adjustment, and Public Assistance.* Washington DC: National Academy Press.

Hernandez, M. (1999). A Profile of Hispanic Americans. Executive Summary. Population Resource Center, Princeton, NJ. [BBB35361]. Sponsored by the Population Resource Center, Washington, D.C.

Hill, J.P. & Holmbeck, G.N.(1986). Attachment and autonomy during adolescence. *Annals of Child Development, 3*, 145-189.

Holmbeck, G.N. (1992). Autonomy and psychological adjustment in adolescence with and without spinea bifida. Paper presented at the Fourth Biennial Meeting of the Society for Research on Adolescence (March), Washington, D.C.

Hondagneu-Sotelo, P. & Avila, E. (1997). I'm here, but I'm there: The meanings of Latina Transnational motherhood. *Gender and Society, 11* (5), 548-571.

Kalff, D. (1980). *Sandplay: A Therapeutic Approach to the Psyche.* Boston: Sigo Press.

Kirkpatrick, L. A. & Shaver, P. R. (1992). An attachment-theoretical approach to romantic love and religious belief. *Personality and Social Psychology Bulletin, 18*, 266- 275.

Kirkpatrick, L. A. & Hazan, C. (1994). Attachment styles and close relationships: A four-year prospective study. *Personal Relationships, 1*, 123-142.

Kobak, R. R. & Hazan, C. (1991). Attachment in marriage: Effects of security and accuracy of working models. *Journal of Personality and Social Psychology, 60*, 861-869

Kroeger, J. (1992). Intrapsychic dimensions of identity during late adolescence. In G.R. Adams, T.P. Gullotta, and R. Montemayor (Eds.). *Adolescent Identity Formation: Advances in Adolescent Development,* vol. 4, Newbury Park, CA: Sage.

Kroeger, J. (1996). *Identity in Adolescence: The Balance Between Self and Other* London and New York: Routledge.

Kurtz, S. N. (1992). *All Mothers are One: Hindu India and the Cultural Reshaping of Psychoanalysis.* New York: Columbia Press.

Linesch, D. G. (1988). *Adolescent Art Therapy.* New York: Brunner/ Mazel.

Lowenthal, D. (1972). *West Indian Societies.* Oxford, England: Oxford University Press.

Mahler, M. S., Pine , F., & Bergman, A. (1975*). The Psychological Birth of the Human Infant.* New York: Basic Books.

Main, M. (1990). Cross-cultural studies of attachment organization: Recent studies, changing methodologies, and the concept of conditional strategies. *Human Development, 33*, 48-61.

Masser, D. (1992). Psychosocial functioning of Central American Refugee Children. Child *Welfare, 71*(5), 439-456.

Maxwell, J. A. (1996). *Qualitative research Design: An Integrative Approach.* Thousand Oaks, CA: Sage Publications.

Mead, M. (1966). A cultural anthropologist's approach to maternal deprivation. In *Deprivation of Maternal Care: A reassessment of its effects.* New York: Schoken Books.

Miyake, K, Chen, S.J., & Campos, J. J. (1985). Infant temperament, mother's mode of interaction, and attachment in Japan. In I. Bretherton and E. Waters (Eds.), *Growing points of attachment theory and research, Monographs of the Society for Research in Child Development, 50*(1-2, Serial number 209), 276-297.

N-Vivo Nud*ist for Qualitative Research (Version 1.0) [Computer Software]. (1999). Australia: QSR – Qualitative Solutions and Research.

Parker, G. (1994). Parental bonding and depressive disorders. In *Attachment in Adults: A Clinical Perspective.* M. Sperling & W. Berman (Eds.). New York: Guilford Press.

Rogers-Mitchell, R. & Friedman, H.S. (1994). *Sandplay: Past, Present and Future.* New York: Routledge.

Roseinstein, D. & Horowitz, H. A. (1996). Adolescent attachment and psychopathology. *Journal of Consulting and Clinical Psychology, 64*(2), 244-253.

Rothenberg, A. (1990). Creativity in adolescence. *Psychiatric Clinics of North America, 13*(3), 415-434.

Ryce-Menuhin, J. (1992). *Jungian Sandplay: The Wonderful Therapy.* New York: Routledge.

Sagi, A., Lamb, M.E., & Lewkowicz, , K.S., Shoham, R., Devir, R., & Estes, D. (1985). Security of infant –mother, -father, and –metapelet attachments among Kibbutz-reared Israeli children. In I. Bretherton and E. Waters (Eds.), *Growing points of attachment theory and rese arch, Monographs of the Society for Research in Child Development, 50*(1-2, Serial number 209), 276-297.

Seidman, I. E. (1991). *Interviewing as qualitative research.* New York: Teachers College Press, Columbia University.

Shaver, P. R. & Brennan, K. A. (1992). Attachment styles and the "big five" personality traits: Their connection with each other and with romantic relationship outcomes. *Personality and Social Psychology Bulletin, 18*, 536- 545.

Shulman, S. & Seiffge, K. I. (1997). *Fathers and Adolescents: A Developmental and Clinical Persepctive.* New York: Routledge.

Sjolund, M. & Schaefer, C. (1994). The Erica method of sandplay diagnosis and assessment. In . K.J. O'Connor & C. E. Shaefer (Eds.). *Handbook of Play Therapy: Advances and Innovations. Vol.2.* NY: John Wiley & Sons, Inc.

Urrutia-Rojas, X., & Rodriguez, N. (1996, December 2). Unnacompanied migrant children from Central-America: *Socio-demographic characteristics and experiences with potentially traumatic events.* Paper presented at the workshop of the ethnographic Research on the Health and Well-Being of Immigrant Children and Families, sponsored by the National Research Council of the Institute of Medicine, Irvine, CA.

Van Ijzendoorn, M. H. (1992). Intergenerational transmission of parenting: A review of studies in non-clinical populations. *Development Review, 12*, 76-99.

Van Ijzendoorn, M. H.; Juffer, F.; & Duyvesteyn, M. G. (1995). Breaking the intergenerational cycle of insecure attachment: A review of the effects of attachment-based interventions on maternal sensitivity and infant security. *Journal of Child Psychology and Psychiatry, 36*(2), 225-248.

Van Ijzendoorn, M. H., & Bakermans-Kranenburg, M. J. (1997). Intergenerational transmission of attachment: A move to the contextual level. In *Attachment and Psychopathology.* L. Atkinson & K. J. Zucker (Eds.). New York: Guilford Press.

Weinrib, E. L. (1983). *Images of the Self.* Boston, MA: Sigo Press.

INDEX